relentless
40 Days in Psalm 119

relentless

40 Days in Psalm 119

Kevin J. Moore, PhD

Foreword by Jimmy Draper

Relentless: 40 Days in Psalm 119

©2016 by Kevin J. Moore

Independently published by the author through Carpenter's Son Publishing, Franklin, Tennessee

Published in association with Larry Carpenter of Christian Book Services, LLC of Franklin, Tennessee

Edited by Gail Fallen

Cover Design by Suzanne Lawing

Interior Layout Design by Adept Content Solutions

ISBN: 978-1-942587-44-6

Printed in the United States of America

Praise for Psalm 119

In keeping with the spirit of *Relentless*, take a moment
and read what others love about Psalm 119.

"The longest Psalm in the Bible has as its focus the ultimate message of heaven to earth. God has spoken and what He has said is trustworthy. That subject is either the bedrock for human society or no such bedrock exists. The only true battle for humankind, past, present, and future, is the issue as to whether man will accept what God has said or reject what He has said."

Bill Anderson, DDiv
Pastor, First Baptist Euless, Texas (1966–1975)
Former Interim Pastor, First Baptist Church, Dallas, Texas (2006–2007)

"I remember two of the first verses I ever memorized in Vacation Bible School were from Psalm 119, verse 11 and verse 105. Even today they are packed with wisdom for living day by day in God-honoring ways. All of Psalm 119 contains more practical strategy than most books I have ever read."

Wes Black, PhD
Author: *An Introduction to Youth Ministry*

"The words of Psalm 119 beautifully express love for God and commitment to the righteous principles revealed in His Word—a hunger and thirst for righteousness that Jesus promises will be satisfied in His kingdom. We need more leaders in our world today who treasure God's Word, trust His wisdom, and delight in His truth as deeply as is described in this wonderful Psalm."

Gary Cook, DMin
President, Dallas Baptist University, Texas

"Psalm 119's instructional journey through the entire Hebrew alphabet reveals just how comprehensively God's Word can transform life, and culture transformations are at the heart of Criswell College's own mission."

Barry Creamer, PhD
President, Criswell College, Dallas, Texas
Professor of Humanities

"Psalm 119 is a gentle but assertive reminder to our visual-dominant culture that God has not given us a movie or show, but a word, more specifically, His Word."

Jason Corn
Discipleship Pastor
Lamar Baptist Church, Arlington, TX

"I love the fact that Psalm 119 is a classic instructional Psalm. By its very design it commends and commands memorization. Memorization of the Word of God allows us to meditate upon and think deeply about the rich wisdom contained therein."

Michael D. Dean, DMin
Senior Pastor, Travis Avenue Baptist Church, Fort Worth, Texas
Author: *Envision the Life: Living God's Unrelenting Vision for Your Life*

"Psalm 119:105 was the very first verse I committed to memory as a new Christian. Since then, the entire chapter has challenged me with its promise that God's Word is the only place we will find ultimate meaning, hope, discernment, and delight. His Word is still 'a lamp for my feet and a light on my path'" (Holman Christian Standard Bible).

Michael Feese, DMin
Senior Pastor, Mount Zion Baptist Church, Alvord, Texas

"Psalm 119 is special because it is a beautiful expression of the joy and delight that comes from meditating on the Word of God. We cannot enjoy the Lord if we refuse to enjoy His Word."

Scott Gray
Senior Pastor, First Baptist Church, Mesquite, Texas

"Psalm 119 is a reminder of the depth, power, and practicality of God's Word. This Psalm challenges me to know and follow God's Word on a daily basis."

Stewart Holloway, PhD
Pastor, First Baptist Church, Pineville, Texas

"May we all be more like the psalmist, transparent about our sin, amazed with the nature of God, and eager to make the Bible the foundation for our life."

Gerre Joiner
Senior Adult Minster, First Baptist Church, Decatur, Texas

"Psalm 119 celebrates the joy and blessing God extends to all who obey the Lord's will as expressed in His Word. The unprecedented repetition of these themes underscores God's earnest offer as well as the human need for continual exhortation to heed the Lord's commands."

George L. Klein, PhD
Professor of Old Testament, Southwestern Baptist Theological Seminary, Fort Worth, Texas
Author: *Zechariah* (New American Commentary)

"The first verse I memorized was Psalm 119:11. Twenty-nine years later, there isn't a week that goes by that I don't meditate on that verse! Time and again, Psalm 119 has been a source of wisdom, guidance, and comfort for me. We challenge our college students to delight themselves in the psalms through prayer and study every semester!"

John Kelsey, DMin
Campus Pastor and Director of the Baptist Collegiate Ministries, University of Oklahoma

"'I pledge allegiance to the Bible, God's holy Word. I will make it a lamp unto my feet, a light unto my path, and will hide its words in my heart, that I may not sin against God.' For countless boys and girls in Vacation Bible Schools across the years, those words from Psalm 119:105 and 119:11 have been a primer on the depth and joy of knowing God's Word. The church needs, as much in this time as any other in history, to hunger for the experience of God through His written self-revelation. Psalm 119 is a treasure for such an experience."

Gerry Lewis, DMin ACC
Executive Director, Harvest Baptist Association, Decatur, Texas
Author: *An Eye on the Harvest*

"Psalm 119 celebrates God's law and we should as well. Jesus was the perfect law keeper and the one who suffered the penalty for disobedience on our behalf. We are not saved by the law, but the law continues to express God's will for how we should love God. I pray that all of us can join the psalmist in his love of God and God's will for our lives."

Tremper Longman III, PhD
Robert H. Gundry Professor of Biblical Studies at Westmont College, Santa Barbara, California
Author: *Psalms: An Introduction and Commentary* (Tyndale Old Testament Commentary)

"What can one rightly say about the significance and the impact of Psalm 119? Its depth and its breadth provide us a road map for a journey to live out the old spiritual song, 'Just a Closer Walk with Thee.'"

Bruce McCoy, DMin
President, Missouri Baptist Convention (2008–2010)
Preaching Representative, Southwestern Baptist Theological Seminary, Fort Worth, Texas

"Psalm 119 challenges me to love God's Word in the practical day-to-day of life. God's promise of 'great peace' for those who love His Law calls believers to regard, meditate upon, never forget, observe, and rejoice in His Word. In these challenging times those who cherish God's Law with their time will have great peace and they will not stumble."

Sha Moore
Chaplain, Wise Choices Pregnancy Resource Center, Decatur, Texas

"While it is almost impossible to pick one 'favorite' when referring to God's Word, Psalm 119 has been one of those 'go to' portions of Scripture since early in my walk with Christ and in my ministry. I read it regularly and often. There is one simple reason: it keeps me focused where I need to be—on the Lord and the absolute truth of His Word. As a pastor, professor, and counselor, God's Word has always been the center of all I do. Psalm 119 reminds me why, and keeps me committed to that."

David Penley, PhD
Professor of Biblical Counseling (Retired)
Southwestern Baptist Theological Seminary, Fort Worth, Texas
Author: *Counseling By the Book*

"Psalm 119 is the mountain peak about God's Word in the Old Testament. Two of the first verses I memorized in my walk with the Lord were 9 and 11. Because of those verses I have returned to this Psalm for almost fifty years to gain strength and direction."

Jim Richards, DMin
Executive Director of the Southern Baptist of Texas Convention
Author: *Revelation: The Best is Yet to Come*

"Psalm 119 was always intimidating to me as a child. I would read through some of the Psalms but would always skip over 119 because it was just too long! Oh, what great truth I missed out on in these early years. This Psalm is such a wonderful testimony of the power of the Word of God. Are we truly relying on it, trusting in it, finding joy in living under it? What a great challenge for me daily—to truly live under the power of the Word of God!"

Joel Skinner
Africa Inland Mission

"Psalm 119 teaches God's people the importance of knowing the eternal truths in His Word so that obedient living is possible. The church can't make disciples of the nations unless His Word is taught faithfully to people who are daily in His Word. As a young father, Psalm 119 was a challenge that pointed me to daily Bible study and teaching my children the Bible so they could live armed against the untruths in the world."

Drew Stasio
Bible Study Fellowship Teaching Leader, Arlington, Texas

"Memorizing Scripture propels young believers toward Christian maturity. 'Hiding God's Word in your heart' is a key tool in my ministry to young adults. There are few spiritual disciplines that bear as much fruit in one's life as memorizing Scripture."

Gary Stidham
Director of the Baptist Student Ministry, The University of Texas at Arlington

"It is through the study of God's Word that my life has been changed and my understanding of our high and almighty God has been expanded. I am struck with the beauty of how this Psalm communicates our utter dependence on God. Only from God do we receive teaching, direction, wisdom, and insight. Only from God do we receive the strength and power to apply all that He reveals to us. Only from God do we receive satisfaction with knowing His unfailing love. Psalm 119 echoes the desires of our hearts as we seek to know, follow, understand, love, and obey our God throughout our time on earth."

Lori Turner
Bible Study Fellowship Teaching Leader, Arlington, Texas

"More often than any place in Scripture, Psalm 119 reminds me that God closely associates His Word with Himself. Psalm 119 has led me to increasingly delight in, love, cherish, meditate on, obey, and remember God and His Word. I pray that by deliberate study of the psalmist's devotion to God and His Word, the Spirit of Christ will stir our hearts to do the same."

Dallas Vandiver
Spiritual Life Coordinator, Christian Academy of Louisville, Kentucky
PhD Student, Southern Baptist Theological Seminary, Louisville, Kentucky

Contents

Dedication xviii
Acknowledgments xix
Foreword by Jimmy Draper xxi
Introduction 1

Day   ***Stanza***
Day 1   א
      Morning Devotional: "Real Blessing" vv. 1–2 7
      Evening Prayer: "Exceeding Obedience" vv. 3–4 9

Day 2   א
      Morning Devotional: "Oh That My Ways . . ." vv. 5–6 11
      Evening Prayer: "Joy in Learning" vv. 7–8 13

Day 3   ב
      Morning Devotional: "The Pure Way" vv. 9–10 15
      Evening Prayer: "Hiding God's Word" vv. 11–16 17

Day 4   ג
      Morning Devotional: "God's Strangers" vv. 17–19 19
      Evening Prayer: "A Wasting Soul" v. 20 21

xiv

Day 5   ג

Morning Devotional: "Arrogance" vv. 21–23 23

Evening Prayer: "My Delight and My Counsel" v. 24 25

Day 6   ד

Morning Devotional: "Clinging to Dust" v. 25 27

Evening Prayer: "You Answered Me" v. 26 29

Day 7   ד

Morning Devotional: "Make Me" vv. 27–29 31

Evening Prayer: "Running Recklessly" vv. 30–32 33

Day 8   ה

Morning Devotional: "To the End" vv. 33–35 35

Evening Prayer: "Turn My Eyes" vv. 36–40 37

Day 9   ו

Morning Devotional: "Taunts" vv. 41–43 39

Evening Prayer: "The Broad Place" vv. 44–45 41

Day 10   ו

Morning Devotional: "Shameless" v. 46 43

Evening Prayer: "Raised Hands" vv. 47–48 45

Day 11   ז

Morning Devotional: "My Comfort" vv. 49–52 47

Evening Prayer: "My Song" vv. 53–56 49

Day 12   ח

Morning Devotional: "My Portion" vv. 57–59 51

Evening Prayer: "Quickly" v. 60 53

Day 13   ח

Morning Devotional: "Midnight" vv. 61–62 55

Evening Prayer: "Friends" vv. 63–64 57

Day 14   ט

Morning Devotional: "Affliction" vv. 65–71 59

Evening Prayer: "Better than Gold" v. 72 61

Contents

Day 15   י
     Morning Devotional: "His Hands" v. 73 63
     Evening Prayer: "A Beautiful Sight" v. 74 65

Day 16   י
     Morning Devotional: "Love" vv. 75–77 67
     Evening Prayer: "Falsely Accused" vv. 78–80 69

Day 17   כ
     Morning Devotional: "Gloriously Faint" vv. 81–82 71
     Evening Prayer: "In the Smoke" v. 83 73

Day 18   כ
     Morning Devotional: "Facing Death" vv. 84–87 75
     Evening Prayer: "Live to Obey" v. 88 77

Day 19   ל
     Morning Devotional: "In the Heavens" vv. 89–91 79
     Evening Prayer: "If Not" v. 92 81

Day 20   ל
     Morning Devotional: "I Am Yours" vv. 93–95 83
     Evening Prayer: "Limitless" v. 96 85

Day 21   מ
     Morning Devotional: "Surpassing Wisdom" vv. 97–100 87
     Evening Prayer: "My Teacher" vv. 101–102 89

Day 22   מ
     Morning Devotional: "Like Honey" v. 103 91
     Evening Prayer: "Godly Hatred" v. 104 93

Day 23   נ
     Morning Devotional: "Light" vv. 105–106 95
     Evening Prayer: "Willing Offering" vv. 107–108 97

Day 24   נ
     Morning Devotional: "Snare" vv. 109–110 99
     Evening Prayer: "My Inheritance" vv. 111–112 101

Day 25   כ
Morning Devotional: "Double-Minded" v. 113 103
Evening Prayer: "My Shield" v. 114 105

Day 26   כ
Morning Devotional: "Go Away" v. 115 107
Evening Prayer: "Sustain" vv. 116–117 109

Day 27   כ
Morning Devotional: "Discarded" vv. 118–119 111
Evening Prayer: "Trembling" v. 120 113

Day 28   ע
Morning Devotional: "Real" vv. 121–122 115
Evening Prayer: "According to Your Love" vv. 123–125 117

Day 29   ע
Morning Devotional: "It Is Time" v. 126 119
Evening Prayer: "Upright" vv. 127–128 121

Day 30   פ
Morning Devotional: "The Simple" vv. 129–130 123
Evening Prayer: "Panting" v. 131 125

Day 31   פ
Morning Devotional: "Established" vv. 132–134 127
Evening Prayer: "Learning to Weep" vv. 135–136 129

Day 32   צ
Morning Devotional: "Tested" vv. 137–140 131
Evening Prayer: "Despised" vv. 141–144 133

Day 33   ק
Morning Devotional: "Crying Out" vv. 145–147 135
Evening Prayer: "Night Watches" v. 148 137

Day 34   ק
Morning Devotional: "Far" vv. 149–151 139
Evening Prayer: "Near" v. 152 141

Day 35   ר
    Morning Devotional: "Plead My Cause" vv. 153–154 143
    Evening Prayer: "Far from the Wicked" v. 155 145

Day 36   ר
    Morning Devotional: "Many Compassions" vv. 156–158 147
    Evening Prayer: "All" vv. 159–160 149

Day 37   ש
    Morning Devotional: "Deception" vv. 161–163 151
    Evening Prayer: "Great Peace" vv. 164–165 153

Day 38   ש
    Morning Devotional: "Waiting" vv. 166–167 155
    Evening Prayer: "Known to You" v. 168 157

Day 39   ת
    Morning Devotional: "Lips" vv. 169–172 159
    Evening Prayer: "Your Hand" v. 173 161

Day 40   ת
    Morning Devotional: "And I will Praise" vv. 174–175 163
    Evening Prayer: "Lost Sheep" v. 176 165

Next Steps to a Relentless Life 167
Memorizing Psalm 119 171
Translation of Psalm 119 175
Notes 185

*I dedicate this book to the Lord
in gratitude for giving me His perfect Word
and for helping me in my relentless pursuit!*

Acknowledgments

I must express my heartfelt gratitude to Lamar Baptist Church for encouraging me to follow God's call on my life to write. I am blessed to pastor a church that pursues Christ relentlessly through the Bible. I am also very grateful to my wife, Stephanie, for helping me develop ideas and communicate them more effectively. Finally, I want to thank those special family and friends along the way that helped me proofread the manuscript. I am forever grateful for all of their support.

Foreword

This volume is a treasure within a treasure! To read and practice the challenges found here is to rediscover one of the most remarkable passages of Scripture in the Bible. Psalm 119 is a Psalm about God's Word. In nearly every verse, there is a synonym for God's Word. It is referred to as "your Word, His testimony, His ways, your precepts, your statutes, the Lord's instruction, His decrees, your commands, the way of truth," and other similar words. It is a Psalm all about the Word of God.

It is contemporary in its application to us today. The culture of the day in which these words were written is very much like our own day. It was a time of rampant religious skepticism, disgusting apathy, and indifference. The people quickly changed in their actions and attitudes. Their attention span was short. They jumped from one fad to another often. The culture was completely profane. It was a time of great wickedness and evil was everywhere. Sounds like our world, doesn't it!

The psalmist was a young man in that kind of hostile environment. Those around him were hostile to faith and to the things of God. He was often the object of derision, slander, and opposition. He was struggling with life in such hostile surroundings. He could have lapsed into depression or bitterness. Instead, he focused on the Word of God and emerged victorious through it all. He declares that the

Word of God is the source of true happiness and satisfaction. It is with that strong pronouncement that he begins this Psalm. "How happy are those whose way is blameless, who live according to the Lord's instruction. Happy are those who keep His decrees and seek Him with all their heart" (Psalm 119:1-2 Holman Christian Standard Bible).

The book of Psalms is different from the rest of the Bible. The Bible is almost exclusively a message to us from God. It is His truth that is communicated throughout. The book of Psalms is primarily man crying out to God. It is in this Psalm that we learn the sufficiency of God's Word. In these verses we cry out with the psalmist for God's presence and provision. It is through these verses that we realize the treasure we have in the written Word of God.

Kevin Moore has spent much of his adult life immersed in Psalm 119. He has committed it to memory and has had it burned into his heart and soul. He has presented us in these pages a remarkable and significant tool to lead us to do the same. It is in these pages that we dwell on the vital importance and complete integrity and sufficiency of God's Word. Follow these pages on a journey of forty days, and it will become the pattern for a lifetime of blessing.

This is not a philosophical or theoretical book. It is a practical guide for our lives. It gives us a deepening understanding of our relationship with God and of our desperate need to apply His truth in our lives. It is the Word of God that ultimately shows us who God is and who we are in Him. It is a book about God's Word, but also about how best to approach God in prayer. In that way, it brings us into intimate fellowship with the One to whom we belong through Christ.

The only way to fill the emptiness of the human heart, which longs for fulfillment and happiness, is through a growing and deepening intimacy with God. These pages will guide you as you travel the road to that experience. And at the end of these pages, Kevin Moore has a special word about the next steps to a life of relentless pursuit of our God!

This is a treasure within a treasure. This book is a refreshing and compelling volume within the treasure of God's inerrant and sufficient Word to us! It is a journey worth taking and a guide that is certain!

—Jimmy Draper
President Emeritus, LifeWay

Introduction

Following Christ demands a relentless commitment to God's Word. For all the talk of the centrality of Scripture in Christian circles, it is shamefully rare to find people fully committed to His Word. Consequently, biblical ignorance among believers has risen to staggering levels. But to say that biblical ignorance is the problem ignores the more troubling concern that people who claim Christ as Savior do not know Him very well. Jesus said, "My sheep listen to my voice; I know them, and they follow me" (John 10:27 New International Version). Knowing Christ intimately is not possible for those who have disregarded the Bible as an irrelevant religious relic. Even genuine believers will not know the Lord very well if they do not consistently spend time in God's Word. But to cast a stone would be to ignore the years I was undisciplined in my study of God's Word.

Oh, the abundance of joy that flooded my life when I began studying, meditating, and memorizing God's Word in college. Prior to my senior year at the University of Oklahoma, I spent a summer in Aspen, Colorado. Disenchanted with my dreams of becoming a professional musician, I began to spend more and more time in God's Word. Between rehearsals and private lessons, I began the arduous task of committing Psalm 119 to memory. I can remember cramming my pocket-sized Bible into my fly fishing jacket and hiking up into the

beautiful Aspen terrain to fish for brook trout. Over and over I would
recite the glorious verses until they became a part of me. It took me
about a year and a half to memorize all 176 verses. Over the years, I
have returned to Psalm 119 again and again to memorize the verses
forgotten. I cannot think of another endeavor that has wrought more
spiritual fruit in my life. I love God's Word, and I am passionate about
every believer in Jesus Christ experiencing the joy of walking closely
to Jesus Christ through His Word.

The Celebration of *Torah*

What is Psalm 119 all about? What could be so important, that it
took 176 verses to say? You may be tempted at this point to skip right
ahead and begin the devotional, but a quick overview of Psalm 119
will enrich your experience. Psalm 119 is a systematic and detailed
celebration of God's Law (*Torah* in Hebrew). Facing persecution from
his enemies, the psalmist turned to God's Word for hope, comfort,
peace, and strength. The psalmist was so captivated with God's *Torah*
that he summoned every reasonable linguistic resource to describe
the excellence of it. In addition to the Hebrew word *Torah* (תּוֹרָה),
the psalmist employed seven other words fairly interchangeably
throughout Psalm 119: "testimonies" (עֵדוּת), "precepts" (פִּקּוּדִים),
"statute" (חֹק), "commandments" (מִצְוֹת), "judgments" (מִשְׁפָּטִים),
"word" (אִמְרָה), and "word" (דָּבָר). Out of 176 verses, only four do not
include one of these eight words (vv. 84, 90, 121, 132). The celebration
of *Torah* in Psalm 119 is divided into twenty-two stanzas which
correspond to the letters of the Hebrew alphabet. All eight verses of
each stanza begin with one letter of the Hebrew alphabet. From *Alef*
to *Tav*, or A to Z, the psalmist explored the magnificence of God's
Torah. But it was not for the sake of literary artistry that Psalm 119
is arranged in this manner. Instead, the acrostic format serves as a
call for God's people to commit the Psalm to memory. But what is
the *Torah*?

To the original audience, the word *Torah* likely signified the
Pentateuch, or the first five books of the Old Testament.[1] By way of
Christian application, and in light of the completion of the Bible, we
now understand Psalm 119 as a call to walk in obedience to all of
God's Word. As the apostle Paul writes, "All Scripture is God-breathed

and is useful for teaching, rebuking, correcting and training in righteousness so that the man of God may be thoroughly equipped for every good work" (2 Tim. 3:16–17). Thus, every morning devotional and evening prayer encourages faithful obedience to the entire Bible. But it's important not to skip over how the original audience would have understood the concept of *Torah* in Psalm 119.

Psalm 119 encouraged Israel to obey the 613 commandments recorded in the Pentateuch. However, we know from Old Testament history that Israel failed miserably, a failure that we have all shared in. As Paul writes, "for all have sinned and fall short of the glory of God" (Rom. 3:23). The only person to fulfill the requirements of the Old Testament Law was Jesus Christ, who lived the perfect life (Matt. 5:17). Jesus is the only one who has lived the kind of blameless life that Psalm 119 commends (Ps. 119:1, 80). Thus, he died as the perfect, atoning sacrifice for our sins. To study Psalm 119 is to be confronted with the excellence of Jesus Christ, who obeyed perfectly, yet took the penalty of our sins on the cross. Because of His resurrection from the dead and as a result of the empowering presence of the Holy Spirit within believers, we can now walk in a manner pleasing to God. Our churches must be filled with believers relentlessly committed to obeying God's Word!

God's Word and the Church

Churches will experience chaos and disorder when their members have no serious commitment to the Scripture. Well-intentioned Christians can lead their church to the brink of ruin when they do not study God's Word. It is the Bible that instructs believers in how to serve underneath the headship of Jesus Christ. The congregations that manage to avoid open conflict are probably filled with such complacency that they are ambivalent to their poor spiritual condition. In such a climate, fellowship, service, and worship suffer since it is God's Word that teaches us to do all of these things.

When God's people refuse to study the full counsel of God, marriages will be unequipped to handle the normal challenges of life. Stress, fear, and anxiety will cripple people from their calling to serve the Lord. Teenagers will likely plunge into fits of rebellion unless they are opening God's Word on a regular basis. People of all ages will crumble underneath everyday trials and temptations without the strength and encouragement of daily Bible reading. Sin will flourish in the lives of people who have no true commitment to Scripture. Those who are broken, lonely, and hurting will not find consolation in churches full of people who have turned their backs on God's Word. Without a commitment to God's Word, churches run the risk of becoming apostate.

Many churches in our world have already caved underneath the pressure of secular society and adopted the more "acceptable" philosophies of the world around them. Sadly, many of these "churches" teach a false gospel to false believers who worship a god of their own making. In so doing, they have sunken into the moral squalor of the world they were called to save. Without repentance, such a move will eventually prompt the judgment of God. Writing to those who embraced the sexual immorality of Jezebel in the church in Thyatira, Jesus warns, "I will cast her on a bed of suffering, and I will make those who commit adultery with her suffer intensely, unless they repent of her ways. I will strike her children dead. Then all the churches will know that I am he who searches hearts and minds, and I will repay each of you according to your deeds" (Rev. 2:22–23). Without a membership committed to God's Word, churches will utterly fail in their mission to glorify God by making disciples of all nations.

How can you make disciples of all nations and teach people to obey everything Christ commanded if you are not a student of God's Word (Matt. 28:19)? God uses His Word to motivate us in taking the gospel to the ends of the earth. Without God's Word, Christians will never understand the desperation of humanity nor the fact that God is worthy to receive glory from a representation of every tribe, tongue, people, and nation (Rev. 7:9). Nothing in church life can compensate for a deficient attention to God's Word. Brilliant pastors, pristine facilities, and excellent programs will all fail without a relentless commitment to God's Word. Even the most exciting praise and worship will yield little without a passion for the Bible. Fear will also take over without a determination to study God's Word. God's Word helps us stand firm against the enemy's relentless assault (Eph. 6:14). The threat of persecution will incapacitate the church in accomplishing the Great Commission if they are not emboldened by God's Word to be courageous amidst satanic opposition.

Nevertheless, some might say that forty days in Psalm 119 amounts to unnecessary redundancy. Why should we commit so much time and energy to studying a single chapter of the Bible? The most compelling answer to this question lies in Psalm 119:96, "To all perfection I have seen an end, but your commandments are exceedingly broad."[2] In short, there is no end to the majestic beauty of God's Word. If given the rest of eternity, we could never exhaust the glorious riches contained in Psalm 119 or any other portion of Scripture, for that matter. We should also remember that the acrostic format of Psalm 119 was meant to encourage memorization. Isn't it interesting that God intended for His people to memorize the longest Psalm in the book of Psalms? Surely a Psalm designed for memorization deserves more than a passing glance or a cursory reading.

I also see incredible value in the staggering volume of repetition in Psalm 119. Let's not think for a moment that Christians only need to hear things once. It's not enough to hear one time that God loves us; we need to hear it over and over for the rest of our lives. We need to sing about it, learn about it, and be reminded of it. We also need constant reminders of God's mercy, grace, and forgiveness. Likewise, followers of Christ need to be confronted over and over with the importance of God's Word. We need every glorious nuance of the 176 verses of Psalm 119 to assault our prideful independence that keeps us from spending time in God's Word. We need to be fascinated with the majestic wonder of God's Word and to pursue it relentlessly so that we can know Jesus.

Relentless and Spiritual Growth

Relentless is designed for both individual and corporate spiritual growth. *Relentless* will help your small group or discipleship class to develop an insatiable appetite for God's Word. If you plan to lead your church through this study, Charles Redding has written an excellent companion for children, ages 6–12, entitled *Relentless, Too! A 40 Day Journey for Kids.* This companion book tracks verse by verse along with the adult version so that families and churches can experience Psalm 119 together. Imagine people of all ages in your church passionately pursuing Christ in the Bible.

My prayer is that you will never feel the same about God's Word. I pray that you will be forever captivated with the unsearchable riches of the Bible, but not simply for the sake of appreciating it. I pray that your relationship with Jesus Christ will grow exponentially as you seek Him through His Word. I pray that you will grow to love, worship, and serve Jesus Christ with greater faithfulness. I also pray that God will use this faithful obedience to both strengthen His Church and bring salvation to the lost. May the Lord bless your relentless pursuit!

Real Blessing

Blessed are those whose ways are blameless,
who walk according to the law of the Lord.
Blessed are those who keep his testimonies,
with all of their heart they seek him.
—Psalm 119:1–2

A relentless pursuit of Christ leads to a life full of God's blessings. The Bible tells us that God crowns the head of the righteous with blessings (Prov. 10:6). You definitely do not want to miss out on His blessings, because they are vast, powerful, and enduring. But these immeasurable blessings do not always translate into an easy life. If you really just want an easy, comfortable life, the blessed life is not for you. Though filled with the incredible swell of God's blessings, the psalmist faced slander (v. 22), mocking (v. 51), death (v. 87), affliction (v. 92), and distress (v. 143). How can anybody who endures these horrific circumstances talk about God's blessings? Yet, in the midst of his incredible adversity, the psalmist experienced delight (v. 16), freedom (v. 45), courage (v. 46), hope (vv. 49–50), contentment (v. 72), joy (v. 111), and peace (v. 165). The psalmist's blessings were not superficial or circumstantial. They were strong, powerful, and transforming! The key to living in the fullness of these blessings lies in a place that few self-proclaiming Christians look—God's Word.

While plenty of people talk of God's blessings, there seems to be little interest in the inseparable concept of obedience to God's Word. It is easier to talk about "claiming blessings," "sowing seeds for blessings," or "believing God for blessings" than it is to pursue a blameless life. Yet, God blesses those who "walk according to the law of the Lord" and "keep his testimonies with all of their heart." Though God may choose to bless you despite your disobedience, we must not divorce the concept of blessings from obedience to God's Word. The true scope of God's blessings are untapped by those who have no interest in pursuing a closer relationship with Jesus Christ.

Obedience is not some cold, mechanical act whereby you prove yourself worthy of His favor. Instead, it is the by-product of having drawn near to the Lord with all of your heart. To be sure, none of us have the strength, discipline, or ability to live a blameless life without God. I know that I have personally failed miserably to obey the Lord. Yet, the good news of the gospel is that God loves us despite our total sinfulness. God makes us blameless as we trust in the work of Jesus Christ, who died on the cross for our sins. God gives us a blameless heart and empowers us through the Holy Spirit to walk in obedience to Him. The once impossible task of walking in obedience to God becomes a glorious reality! A reality that God intends not just for you personally, but for His church. The blessed life is real, tangible, and available to you today as you pursue Christ relentlessly through His Word.

Exceeding Obedience

They also do no wrong; they walk in his ways.
You have commanded your precepts
to be kept exceedingly.
—Psalm 119:3–4

Father, I confess that your Word is all too often lodged into false categories of optional, seasonal, or non-urgent in my mind. Sometimes I consider my personal agenda to be more pressing than your eternally perfect Word. I will stop everything to satisfy the smallest craving yet procrastinate in doing what I know will bring you glory. I overextend myself in accomplishing nonessentials yet find it difficult to deny my flesh when it comes to obeying your Word.

Yet, you have commanded your Word to me. Your Word is not a suggestion; you commanded it. You commanded your Word not only to me, but to all of my brothers and sisters in Christ. You don't simply want us to appreciate, ponder, or talk about your Word. You want us to obey your Word. You have commanded your people to respond to your Word with "exceeding obedience." You are the Creator of the Ends of the Earth and the Savior of the World. You are worthy of more than the languid obedience that I so often give you. Lord, forgive me for denying you the exceeding obedience that you deserve.

Father, thank you for your forgiveness made possible through the life, death, and resurrection of your Son. Help me to rest tonight in the knowledge of your total forgiveness. Thank you for helping me to live in exceeding obedience to your Word by the power of your Holy Spirit. No matter how confusing my life becomes, I know that walking in obedience to your Word is always right. Help me to awake tomorrow with an earnest desire to walk in exceeding obedience to your Word. Give me strength to set an obedient example for my brothers and sisters in Christ. Thank you, Lord, for the blessings that await me!

Oh That My Ways …

Oh that my ways may be established
to keep your statutes.
Then I would not be ashamed
when I consider all of your commandments.
—Psalm 119:5–6

God wants to help you in your relentless pursuit of Him. You cannot obey God's Word without God's help. My sheer determination to obey God on my own will never overpower the cravings of my flesh or the evil one's desire to entangle me in sin. In fact, without God's help my best attempts at obedience will invariably inflame my desire to rebel against Him. Fortunately, God longs to "establish" you and me in a life of obedience. Interestingly, the word "establish" in Psalm 119 refers to things that only God does, like creation itself (vv. 73, 90, 133). It is as though the psalmist is saying, "Just as you created me in your image and fashioned the heavens to endure, make my obedience real and lasting." The God who created the universe wants to establish your life in His Word. Discipline yourself to study God's Word, but never trust in your own ability to obey.

One of the most wonderful things about God establishing your life in obedience is that you can avoid the shame that accompanies sin. Obedience to God's Word always prompts us to love and adore Jesus more. But disobedience causes us to feel a sense of shame when we remember how God told us to live. All Christians have temporarily felt the sting of shame when they disobey God's Word. Thankfully, as we turn from sin, the disgrace turns to joy as we remember that Christ bore the shame for all of our sin. As the Scripture promises, "the one who believes in him will never be put to shame" (Rom. 9:33). God wants to establish you in a life free from the sting of shame.

A life of radical obedience to the Lord is never just an individual pursuit. We all need our brothers and sisters in Christ. God wants to establish His church in His Word. Maybe it's time to surround yourself with others who are daily praying, "Oh that my ways may be established to obey your statutes ..." Consider all of the areas in your life where you have experienced victory and help others with what you learned. But let's not forget to be learners as well. Learn from those who have gained victory in areas where you still struggle. As we strive together to please the Lord, we can celebrate the One who bore our shame on the cross. What a joy it is to raise our voices in celebration of the God who trampled our sin and hurled it into the depths of the sea (Mic. 7:19). What a delight it is to praise the God, who separated our sins from us "as far as the east is from the west" (Ps. 103:12). May God strengthen and unite His children as He establishes us in His Word.

Joy in Learning

I will praise you with an upright heart
as I learn your righteous judgments.
I will keep your statutes;
do not totally forsake me.
—Psalm 119:7–8

Father, I praise you for giving me an upright heart because I trust in the work of your Son for the forgiveness of my sins! I praise you for liberating me from shame, guilt, and slavery to sin. I rejoice that I am free to love you, free to serve you, and free to learn your Word. I thank you for the joy that comes as I study your Word. I sense your presence when I learn new things in your Word. My heart erupts with the highest praise when you quicken my mind to understand your Word. I rejoice over your power, your mercy, and your grace in the Scripture. I rejoice in learning of your faithfulness, your love, and your goodness to me. The more I see the sinfulness and depravity of this world, the more I grieve, but the more I learn about you, the more I rejoice.

Father, there is so much I have to learn in your Word. Guard me from the sin of thinking that my understanding of your Word is complete. Help me not to squander the precious time you give me to spend in your Word. Help me to seize opportunities throughout the remainder of this week to seek you through your Word. When I am tempted to waste my time in meaningless ways, thank you for drawing me close to you through your Holy Spirit. I know that my joy in Christ will be proportional to the time I spend with you through your Word.

Father, I commit to keeping your Word, but I beg for you to help me! I cannot keep your Word unless you help me. Thank you, Lord that you will never leave or forsake me (Deut. 31:6). Thank you for your presence with me as I seek to live a repentant life. Thank you for accompanying me in the journey of living differently from the lost world. Help me to rise tomorrow with a great zeal for you and your Word.

The Pure Way

How can a young man keep his way pure?
By keeping it according to your word.
With all of my heart I have sought you;
do not let me stray from your commandments.

—Psalm 119:9–10

Every believer in Christ can pursue the Lord relentlessly, regardless of age. Do not accept the inevitability of rebellion in young people. Scripture never grants young people a license to rebel; thus, it should never be an expectation of anybody in the church. Nevertheless, our culture scarcely expects any maturity or productivity before the mid to late twenties. Instead of accepting the unbiblical expectation of moral recklessness in young people, we should challenge them to emulate the extraordinary examples of young men like Josiah and David in the Scripture.

As a young man, King Josiah sought the Lord and purged Judah of the idolatry. He tore down the altars to Baal and smashed the idols and Asherah poles. He courageously took the remains of these altars and scattered them on the graves of those who sacrificed to them (2 Chron. 34:3–7). His zeal for the Lord dwarfs the anemic commitment of many believers who have known Christ for years. We see the same zeal for the Lord in the life of David, whose faith incited him to threaten a well-armed giant named Goliath. With unrestrained abandon for God, David challenged Goliath, saying, "You come against me with sword and spear and javelin, but I come against you in the name of the LORD Almighty, the God of the armies of Israel, whom you have defied. This day the LORD will deliver you into my hands, and I'll strike you down

and cut off your head. This very day I will give the carcasses of the
Philistine army to the birds and the wild animals, and the whole world
will know that there is a God in Israel" (1 Sam. 17:45–46). So we know
it's possible for young people to passionately serve the Lord, but how
can they keep their way pure in such a depraved world?

This very question is raised by Job's "friends" in Job 15:14 and
25:4, but for a different reason. Eliphaz and Bildad ask the question to
ridicule the notion that somebody could live in a blameless manner
before God, whereas the psalmist asks the question in order to teach
his audience how it's done. Since God has given you a clean heart
through the life, death, and resurrection of Jesus Christ, you can
pursue the blameless life by the power of the Holy Spirit. When you
come to God through faith in Christ, the Spirit of Christ helps you
crave that which is pleasing to the heavenly Father (Phil. 2:13).

A pure life is ultimately not about pleasing one's teacher, coach,
or student pastor by trying to master a complex matrix of dos and
don'ts; every attempt at this will end in burnout or failure. In the
same way, a pure life is not simply about avoiding a criminal record.
All Christians young and old can live a pure life only as they walk in
obedience to God's Word. Obeying God's Word is not a result of your
determination, but a result of your relationship with Him. As we grow
closer to the Lord, we want to obey Him. In the same way, the more we
obey Him the more we long to know Him. As you seek the Lord with
all of your heart, you can trust God to help you stay on the right path.

With all of my heart, I wish that I had spent my time as a youth
relentlessly pursuing Christ. I will never be able to get back the time
I wasted during my teenage years. Though I cannot change the past, I
can invest my life in the next generation of young people. How might
God use you to do the same? Would you pray regularly for teenagers
in your church? Would you devote your time to cultivating passionate
followers of Christ? Would you model a relentless commitment to
Christ for the young people in your church? May it not be said of us
that we raised a generation, "who knew neither the LORD nor what he
had done for Israel" (Judg. 2:10).

Hiding God's Word

I have laid up your word in my heart so that I will not sin against you.
Blessed are you, Oh Lord, teach me your statutes.
With my lips I recount all of the judgments of your mouth.
I rejoice in the way of your testimonies as much as in all of the riches.
I will meditate on your precepts and I will consider your ways.
I delight in your statutes; I will not forget your word.
—Psalm 119:11–16

Father, thank you for giving your precious Word to me. I confess that I have not devoted myself to the task of internalizing your perfect Word. While ignoring the opportunity to memorize your wonderful Word, I have internalized so many worthless things. I confess that I am so quick to entertain fear, worry, and anxiety. I have internalized anger, bitterness, and jealousy. These sins have made me cold toward you and indifferent toward the world you died to redeem. Thank you for your forgiveness.

Give me an insatiable thirst for your Word. Help me treasure your Word in my heart more than anything else in this life. Help me to seize moments throughout each day to meditate on and delight myself in your Word. As I feed myself on your Word, accomplish everything you desire for me. Work powerfully to conform me into the image of your Son. Transform me by the renewing of my mind (Rom. 12:2). May you equip me to do everything that you have called me to do as I feast on your Word. Teach me to love your church more. Give me an equal desire to show love to a lost world. As I store up your Word within me, compel me to love others with your truth. As I meditate on the beauty of the gospel, teach me to be more faithful in sharing it with others.

Convict me of sin as I internalize your Word. May the presence of your Word within me give me a hatred for pride, strife, greed, and every form of idolatry. May your Word give me a disdain for sexual immorality. Give me strength to put sin to death so that I don't cause my brothers and sisters in Christ to stumble. Produce holiness and joy within me as I feast on your Word. Equip me to bring you the glory that you deserve.

God's Strangers

Deal kindly with your servant
and I will live and I will keep your word.
Open my eyes that I may see the wonders of your law.
I am a stranger on earth;
do not hide your commandments from me.

—Psalm 119:17–19

Your relentless obedience to God's Word will make you a stranger to the world around you. Whereas most people are desperate to fit in, believers are called to pursue a life that will make them increasingly different from the world around them. Amidst the vast ocean of people clamoring for money, influence, pleasure, and worldly gain, a very small minority of committed Christians are praying, "Deal kindly with your servant and I will keep your word." Amidst the deafening selfishness of a lost world, you can scarcely hear saints praying, "Open my eyes that I may see the wonders of your law." These cries, though foreign to a lost world, are sweet in the ears of Almighty God. God has always had a special love for those who cried out to Him, "I am a stranger on earth."

Abraham made the very same declaration as the psalmist after leaving his home in Ur (Gen. 23:4). At God's command, Abraham left everything that was familiar to him to travel to a new home that the Lord prepared for him (Gen. 12:1–5). All of Abraham's descendants took on the identity of a stranger as they experienced four hundred years of captivity in Egypt. Even after their deliverance from Egypt, the Israelites wandered as strangers in the wilderness for forty years. As they journeyed through the wilderness, God showed His love for them by providing for their needs. But God's love for strangers extended beyond the descendants of Abraham. God repeatedly expressed His concern for non-Israelites like Ruth, who chose to identify with the Lord: "Your people will be my people and your God my God" (Ruth 1:16). And still today, God cares about every person who chooses to be a stranger to the world.

Draw near to God through His Word and become increasingly strange to this lost world (Heb. 11:13). Be a stranger to the idolatry and unbridled lust for worldly possessions that surround you. Be a stranger to the voracious appetite for leisure and unholy entertainment.

Be a stranger to all of the "sinful desires, which wage war against your soul" (1 Pet. 2:11). Fan the flame of your love for God and suffocate your desires for the sinfulness of this world (1 John 2:15). Living as a citizen of heaven (Phil. 3:20), however, will not endear you to a lost world. In fact, some may even hate you because of your love for Jesus (1 John 3:13). But, that does not mean that you have to be lonely and deprived of meaningful relationships.

As you abstain from the evil of this world, surround yourself with other strangers journeying toward their heavenly home (John 14:1–3). Find best friends, brothers, sisters, fathers, and mothers in the body of Christ. Join with those who will love you, encourage you, and pray for you. Partner with them to pierce the pervasive darkness of this world with the light of the gospel. Nestled in the warmth and strength of a Christian community, you will be able to endure the alienation of a lost world.

The joy of being a stranger to the world, though, is rooted in the fact that you are known intimately by the only One that matters: the Savior of the world. If you have trusted Jesus Christ for the forgiveness of your sins, you have come to know the One who knew and loved you before you were born (Jer. 1:5; Ps. 139). As you grow more and more foreign to this perishing world, relish every opportunity to know and be known by your God!

A Wasting Soul

*My soul wastes with longing
for your judgments at all times.*
—Psalm 119:20

Father, I am a stranger on earth and you are the only one that truly satisfies me. Although I know I cannot find satisfaction in the pleasures of this world, forgive me for all of the ways in which I try. I have repeatedly tried to fill the longings of my heart with things that cannot satisfy. Help me see the folly of every vain pursuit. Crush the fleshly sense of independence and self-sufficiency that keep me from seeking you through your Word. As you purge my covetous desires, grant me a soul that wastes with longing for your judgments.

May every moment spent in your Word spark a desire for more. Cause the pages of your Word to invigorate a relentless desperation for you. Grant me an insatiable appetite for your judgments at all times. Please show me the ways in which I squander my time. Help me to see every day as an opportunity to pore over the pages of your perfect Word.

Give me a holy concern for my brothers and sisters in Christ as I seek you through your Word. Help me to grow with other Christians in my love for your Word. I pray that my love for your Word would ignite a passion for Bible study in the hearts of my brothers and sisters in Christ.

When I awake tomorrow, help me to act on my desperation for you, by opening your Word. Guard my heart from the temptation to rush into the responsibilities and pressures of my day before spending meaningful time with you in your Word. May even the frailest attempt to spend time with you in the morning be met with an abundance of joy and peace. After spending time in your Word, help me to face every challenge with courage, faith, and strength. Thank you for granting me a soul that wastes with longing for your judgments.

Arrogance

You rebuke the arrogant who are cursed,
who stray from your commandments.
Remove from me shame and contempt,
for I have kept your testimonies.
Even though rulers sit and speak against me,
your servant will meditate on your statutes.

—Psalm 119:21–23

Straying from God's Word is never harmless. Ignoring God's Word is always a brazen act of arrogance. Those who reject God's Word are saying by their actions that they have no need to hear from the God who spoke creation into being. Those who reject God's Word are also saying that they do not need the eternal wisdom of God, who protects, guides, and comforts. The most egregious arrogance, however, is acting as though they have no need of a savior, no need for God's love or the blood of Jesus Christ. Those who live in intentional and habitual rebellion are "cursed." That is, they live underneath the consequences of their wickedness from a just and righteous God.

All of us are acquainted with the sting of insults. Maybe you can still remember the painful things said about you growing up. As painful as these comments can be, they are still just words spoken by insecure peers. Rarely are their words accompanied by the threat of bodily injury. But imagine for a moment that the most powerful rulers have gathered together for the purpose of maligning you because of your fidelity to God's Word. This is what the psalmist endured. The emotional duress caused by the credible threat to his personal safety must have been crippling. Yet the psalmist remained steadfast in meditating on God's Word.

Our whimsical approach to God's Word pales in comparison to the psalmist's incredible faithfulness. Literally anything can keep us from spending meaningful time in God's Word. A bad day at work, a restless night, a favorite television show, or even the mildest of challenges might derail us from spending time in the Bible. It's also easy to drop our daily devotions while vacationing or away from home on business. Homework, fatigue, and responsibilities can easily become excuses for not zealously seeking a closer relationship with Christ through His Word. As for me, I am very proficient at rationalizing away my slothfulness in God's Word. I can even come up with religious reasons for why it's not practical for me to feast on God's Word. How can we expect to stand firm in our faith in this increasingly evil world when we are so easily sidetracked? If the most powerful people in our country assembled for the purpose of slandering you, would you still study God's Word?

As you begin your day, be mindful of the temptation to allow ordinary struggles to keep you from studying God's Word. Instead of using everyday trials as excuses to neglect your study of God's Word, let them serve as reminders of your desperation for Jesus. Start small if you like, but start. What if you read and meditated on just one verse every day? Give God ten minutes a day, and see what happens. I believe that God will captivate you with His glory and leave you with a voracious appetite for more of Him!

My Delight and My Counsel

*Your testimonies are my delight,
my counselors.*
—Psalm 119:24

Father, your testimonies are more delightful than the finest things this world has to offer. Nothing I could ever buy compares with what you have spoken to me in your Word. Teach me to delight every day in your Word.

Thank you for counseling me through your Word. Even my most trusted confidants are capable of rendering bad advice, but your Word will never lead me astray. Even if I could summon advice from the wisest people on the planet, no counsel could surpass the inestimable worth of your Word.

I confess that I lack direction in life as a result of not seeking you through your Word. Through your Word, you have made it abundantly clear how to live a life glorifying to you.

I confess that my emotions and feelings all too often determine my actions. Teach me to obey your Word no matter how it feels.

I confess that I am too quick to turn to my opinions when faced with questions. Help me to assess the worth of every opinion based upon how it aligns with Scripture.

I confess that I have all too often followed the example of those around me instead of yielding to your Word. Help me pattern my life after Jesus Christ.

Grant me grace as I strive to improve my understanding of your Word. May your Holy Spirit illuminate your Word to me—not so that I can be puffed up with knowledge, but so that I can know and understand the way in which I need to walk. Apply your Word to areas of my life where I am not sure what to do. Help me to see every situation through the lens of your truth.

After you have counseled me, grant me grace to obey your perfect wisdom. Guard me from the sin of ignoring your counsel. Help me to awake in the morning ready to measure every decision against the truth of your Word.

Clinging to Dust

My soul clings to the dust;
give me life according to your word.
—Psalm 119:25

Sometimes, the frailty of our humanity overwhelms us. God formed us from the dust and to dust each of us will one day return (Eccles. 3:20). As dust reacts instantly to the gentlest wafts of air, so our weak frames tremble at the faintest problems in life. Even the most ordinary challenges can leave us feeling out of control and helpless. Maybe you have experienced this lately. Sometimes the stress of a wounded relationship or a financial problem can make us miserable. It takes very little to drive most of us to the point of desperation.

Despite our weaknesses, we tend to try and fix our problems. So, we dutifully worry about them hoping that this will produce a solution. But these frantic attempts always seem to end in frustration. After exhausting all of our futile efforts to unscramble our unrelenting pressures, we despair. In our despair we are tempted to numb our angst with vain trivialities, a strategy that only temporarily masks the pain. Over time, however, feelings of bitterness or anger slowly begin to seep out of our frustration. But everything changes when we look for life in God's unchanging Word.

Plagued by the slander of rulers, the psalmist cried out, "Give me life according to your word," not once, but over and over (vv. 37, 40, 88, 107, 149, 154, 156, 159). To many, the psalmist's predicament presented precisely the worst time to sit down and study God's Word.

Yet this kind of objection underscores just how little people esteem God's Word. Mired in the dust of our humanity, God's Word gives life. What else could a man overwhelmed by the dust of his humanity do? Those who feel completely overwhelmed by their total inability to fix their situation must "cling" to God's Word for life. Turning to the Bible in the midst of problems is a powerful acknowledgment in the strength of Almighty God, whose power is "made perfect in weakness" (2 Cor. 12:9). God will prove Himself to be an eternal rock of strength to those who are ready to admit the dust of their humanity.

Drawing near to God through His Word brings life because you encounter the fullness of the God of life in the pages of Scripture. Not only does God create life, He also powerfully sustains life through every conceivable adversity. God redeems those who trust in Jesus from the insatiable appetite of the grave and gives them eternal life. God gives abundant life to those who know and love Jesus Christ (John 10:10). God's Word also teaches us about Christ's victory over Satan, the one who destroys life. But we will never turn to God's Word if we think we are self-sufficient.

You have no life apart from the Lord. Prior to salvation, you were dead in your transgressions and deserving of God's wrath (Eph. 2:1). In light of this chilling reality, do not try to find life outside of Christ. Cry out to God for life and seek Him in His Word! Set an example for your brothers and sisters in Christ by refusing to despair in the midst of your trial. Demonstrate an unflinching faith in the Author of Life by seeking Him relentlessly in His Word (Acts 3:15)! When your life ebbs toward the dust from which you came, God's Word gives life.

You Answered Me

*I have recounted my ways
and you answered me;
teach me your statutes.*

—Psalm 119:26

You are a loving Father who answers every prayer. On my worst days, you have answered me and come to my aid. When fear gripped me, you gave me courage. When rejection brought despair, you gave me peace that surpasses understanding (Phil. 4:7). When I was lonely, you surrounded me with your presence. When my mind was saturated in anxiety, you gave me boldness. In frustration and anger, you brought me calm. When I was discouraged over my sin, you helped me receive your grace. When I was confused, you gave me direction. When I failed, you gave me strength to keep moving. When I was under attack, you dealt with my oppressor. When I was incapacitated with fatigue, you gave me rest. When I faced immovable obstacles, you moved mountains. When I was sad, you comforted me. When I was sick, you sustained me and gave me health.

In the most creative and unexpected ways, you have demonstrated to me that you hear me. Sometimes, in ways that nobody else would recognize, you remind me that you listen and respond to my prayers. You answer even the prayers that are relatively small and inconsequential to the overall scheme of things. You always answer.

Despite your perfect faithfulness, I confess that I sometimes question whether or not you will respond to my prayers. Such doubt makes me lax and unfaithful in my prayer life. Father, forgive me for doubting your goodness and faithfulness. Forgive me for not entrusting more things to you in prayer. Give me grace to bring more requests to you, knowing that you always listen. Teach me your statutes so that I can learn to trust you more with every need I have.

Tonight, as I lie down, help me rest with the knowledge that you have heard my prayers. Help me to sleep knowing that you are powerful. Tomorrow, help me to awake with a renewed trust in your power to answer every prayer.

Make Me

*Make me understand the way of your precepts
and I will meditate on all of your wonders.*

*My soul weeps from sorrow;
strengthen me according to your word.*

*Put away from me the way of deception;
give me life according to your law.*

—Psalm 119:27–29

Do you remember the simple pleasure of being able to raise your hand in class and ask the teacher any question that you had? We were told repeatedly that there was "no such thing as a stupid question." And no matter what we asked, there was always a teacher to give us answers. As we get older, though, it becomes harder to find somebody who can answer the complicated questions of life. But followers of Jesus can still raise their hands. In Jeremiah 33:3, the Lord says to Israel, "Call to me and I will answer you and tell you great and unsearchable things you do not know." Like the psalmist, we can raise our voice to the Lord and say, "make me understand."

The psalmist's persistent calls for understanding (vv. 18, 27, 33–36, 73, 144, 169) convey an unusual desperation for God's Word. Such desperation is relatively foreign to those who have succumbed to the temptation to think of the Bible as just another "interesting religious book." Indifference to God's Word often keeps people from asking for understanding, and the ignorance that ensues only feeds the insidious ambivalence that began the cycle. Those who know the Lord, however, will live their lives praying, "make me understand the way of your precepts."

Do you ask God for help in your study of the Scripture? Sometimes we approach the Bible in such a perfunctory manner that we do not even think to ask God for help. Yet consider for a moment just how motivated God would be to answer our desperate cries for insight. Perhaps our time in God's Word would be punctuated with the same cries for understanding if we grasped just how wonderful the Bible really is.

God's Word is not simply a repository of helpful hints on how to conduct a successful life. Never reduce the Bible to a mere collection of interesting historical facts and useful sayings. God's Word is an infinitely glorious fountain of wonders. In the Scripture we come face to face with the God who created everything from nothing. We encounter God's love for humanity and His desire to redeem them through the work of the cross. We witness God's power to defeat sin and death through the resurrection of Christ from the dead. Through the pages of the Bible, our glorious God speaks life into our sorrow. You cannot stand to miss out on the blessing of understanding His wondrous Word.

Call out to Him today for understanding! Beg like a pauper for God to open your mind to how His revealed character in the Scripture responds to every need you have. Turn from your self-reliance as you study God's Word. Lean on the Holy Spirit to guide you into all truth (John 16:13). May our glorious God permeate churches that resound with saints crying out, "make me understand…" May the world see the transforming power of our glorious Lord in the lives of those who have learned to pray, "make me understand …"

"Oh, the depth of the riches of the wisdom and knowledge of God!
How unsearchable his judgments, and his paths beyond tracing out!"
—Romans 11:33

Running Recklessly

I have chosen the way of faithfulness;
I have set your judgments before me.
I cling to your testimonies, Oh Lord,
do not let me be put to shame.
I run in the path of your commandments,
for you have broadened my heart.
—Psalm 119:30–32

Father, I have chosen the way of faithfulness; I have set your Word before me. Thank you for drawing me to yourself through your Holy Spirit. Thank you for opening my eyes and helping me to understand that your Son died on the cross for my sins and that you raised Him from the dead to give me eternal life. By your grace, I have determined that I want to follow you and serve you for the rest of my life. Tonight, Lord, I commit myself fully and totally to you.

Tonight, I cling to the promise that I am forgiven. I cling to the truth that I am never alone. I cling to the assurance that you will protect me and give me strength to serve you. As I cling to your Word, you will never let me be put to shame. Thank you, Lord, for upholding me in every conceivable way as I serve you with all of my heart.

I confess I have strayed times without number. I have wandered from your perfect Word and clung to my own self-sufficiency. At times, I have clung to my experience and my abilities more than your Word. Father, forgive me for these sins. Take my restless energy and focus it toward your Word. Redirect my passions and desires in the direction of your Word. Harness my vigor for your Word.

Tomorrow, please help me to run with reckless abandon in the path of your commandments. All of my selfish pursuits are a waste of time. But running in the path of your commandments brings me life, joy, and freedom. Lord, help me remember to run this race with my brothers and sisters in Christ. Give me grace to encourage others to run in the path of your Word! Help me not to leave my Christian brothers and sisters behind. Cause your church to run in the path of your commandments!

Day 8 — Morning

To the End

*Teach me, Oh Lord, the way of your statutes
and I will keep them to the end.*

*Give me understanding and I will keep your law
and obey it with all of my heart.*

*Lead me in the path of your commandments,
for in them I delight.*

—Psalm 119:33–35

We live in a day of temporary commitments. We rarely make commitments that will require significant amounts of energy for long periods of time. Instead, we commit ourselves to ministries that will be over in six to eight weeks or sometimes in a single day. We assume positions of leadership within the church only because we know that the term is limited. Our selfish desire to have others minister to us, in conjunction with our unwillingness to persevere through difficult circumstances, render us hesitant to commit to anything that does not have a clear terminus in sight. But does our Christian life resemble the sort of relentless commitment that Christ deserves? What if there was no end in sight?

Would you still commit to something if you knew it would require everything you are and everything you have for the rest of your life? This is the essence of the Christian life and a litmus test for those who claim to know the Lord. Placing your faith in Christ represents the beginning of an eternal commitment to obey and worship the Lord Jesus Christ. As the author of Hebrews stressed, "We have come to share in Christ, if we indeed hold our original conviction firmly to the very end" (Heb. 3:14). Christ Himself conveyed this truth when He said, "the one who stands firm to the end will be saved" (Mark 13:13). Jesus did not give Simon and Andrew a temporary assignment when they dropped their nets to follow Jesus. It's not as though they were agreeing to a short stint as itinerant preachers. There were no exclusion clauses in their "contract" with the Lord that would provide a convenient exit while under duress, danger, or persecution. Jesus said, "follow me" (Matt. 4:19), and the disciples followed.

The psalmist's commitment to the Lord is unimpeachable. Notice that his unending commitment to the Lord is inseparable from his longing to know God's Word. Ignorance of God's Word will always strangle the allegiance of those who say they want to follow Jesus. Those who are relentlessly faithful to the Lord have learned to pray along with the psalmist, "Teach me, Oh Lord, the way of your statutes." But what is motivating him to obey the Lord in verse 35?

Delight. It is the prospect of "delight" that drives his commitment to obey with all of his heart to the end. The prospect of delight will always outperform the highest degrees of self-discipline and determination. Without delighting in God's Word, your commitment to obey the Lord will eventually shrivel away. Remember, "the joy of the LORD is your strength" (Neh. 8:10). Do not underestimate the power of delighting in God's Word.

Your commitment to God must never be seasonal, intermittent, or conditional. Perish the thought that your pursuit of Christ can be anything but permanent. Your commitment to follow Christ unconditionally must be accompanied by a concern for your brothers and sisters in Christ. The command to "hold unswervingly to the hope we profess" cannot be separated from the responsibility to "consider how we may spur one another on toward love and good deeds" (Heb. 10:23–24). As you strive to maintain your commitment to the Lord, though, rest under the promise that God will keep you strong to the end so that you will be "blameless on the day of our Lord Jesus Christ" (1 Cor. 1:8).

Exceeding Obedience

Incline my heart to your testimonies and not to selfish gain.
Turn my eyes from seeing worthless things and give me life in your ways.
Establish your word to your servant that you may be feared.
Take away my disgrace which I dread, for your judgments are good.
See how I long for your precepts; in your righteousness, give me life.
—Psalm 119:36–40

Lord, you are more beautiful than words can express. There is nothing in this life that compares with the deep joy I have in your presence. Every longing finds fulfillment in you. Your goodness, grace, and power overwhelm me with such contentment. Every moment with you reveals the vanity of so many things that I give myself to.

My heart is so prone toward folly. I confess the ways in which I gave myself toward emptiness today. Every moment spent in earthly vanity robs me of joy in you. My sin also weakens my resolve to spread your fragrance to a dying world. By faith in the work of Jesus, I receive your forgiveness and trust that you have made me righteous. In my own strength I cannot maintain my focus on you.

Incline my heart toward your Word and not toward selfish gain. Seize all of my sinful desires and help me focus on you. Keep me from the love of money and from the gnawing covetousness that surrounds me. Turn my eyes away from every worthless thing that creates an insatiable appetite for more vanity. Help me despise the things of this earth that grieve you. Establish your truth within me so that I might live in holy reverence toward you. Take away the disgrace that comes from living for the world and help me to see the goodness of your Word.

May my life cause others to crave your presence and despise sin. Discipline my eyes so that my mind will be filled with your life-giving truth. I pray that my focus on you would create new desires that can only be satisfied by more of you. Consume my life with an intense desire for you. Help my eyes to see all that is beautiful in your Word and all that is worthless in this world. Thank you for helping me awake with a fresh determination to gaze upon your beauty and to seek you.

"One thing I ask of the Lord, *this is what I seek:*
that I may dwell in the house of the Lord *all the days of my life,*
to gaze upon the beauty of the Lord *and to seek him in his temple."*
—Psalm 27:4

Taunts

May your steadfast love come to me, Oh Lord,
your salvation according to your word.
Then I will give an answer to the one who taunts me,
for I trust in your word.
Do not snatch the word of truth utterly from my mouth,
for I have put my hope in your judgments.
—Psalm 119:41–43

There are real consequences to living a relentless life. To say that the world will not applaud your love and devotion to Jesus is an understatement. They will mock, ridicule, and revile you. They may even threaten to fire or sue you. But for many around the world, the opposition has moved far beyond mere threats and intimidation. Enemies of the cross (Phil. 3:18) have murdered countless Christians. This is the work of Satan, who was hurled out of heaven for slandering "day and night" (Rev. 12:10). Satan is a "liar and the father of lies" (John 8:44). The evil one will assault you with hateful accusations. He may try to haunt you with painful memories of past sins or cause you to doubt God's love and forgiveness. He may subtly whisper his insolent taunts or incite others to condemn you forcefully to your face. But the question is, what can you do when facing the enemy's onslaught?

While facing the torrent of persecution, the psalmist held fast to God's love. God's love obliterates the enemy's attack. It is for this reason that the psalmist cried out, "May your steadfast love come to me, Oh Lord, your salvation according to your word." Not one of the enemy's taunts can survive the majestic love of our Lord.

As you face the enemy's fomenting and defamatory slurs, cling to the love that God expressed through the work of the cross. When the wicked scoff at your faith, respond with joy, knowing that God loves you. If unbelievers malign you because of sinful things you have done in the past, revel in the truth that Jesus took the penalty of your sins already. When you feel ostracized by an ungodly world, enjoy the fellowship of other believers whom Jesus died to redeem. God's love overwhelms the reproach of the wicked.

Feast on the reality of God's love today by seeking Him through His Word. God's Word will teach you all about His love. Do not let God's Word leave your mouth. Ask God to make you indifferent to the enemy's brazen attacks. As you experience victory in this area of your life, pray for your brothers and sisters who are struggling.

The Broad Place

I will keep your law continually,
forever and ever.
I will walk about in a broad place,
for I have sought your precepts.
—Psalm 119:44–45

Father, my heart longs for a place that can only be found in you, a broad place full of peace, joy, and rest. I know that the broad place exists because I have been there with you. I have tasted the sweetness of your presence in this place and know the joy of it (Ps. 84). When I'm there, I experience rest from fear, burdens, and stress. A calm boldness overtakes my naturally frantic efforts that exhaust me. Delight overwhelms the anxiety of my petty trials, leaving me with a peace "that surpasses understanding" (Phil. 4:7).

Shamefully, I have so often forgotten the way to this broad place. I confess that I have looked longingly for this broad place through achievements, possessions, and approval. The fleeting pleasures of this world briefly mask my longing for you but always leave me with gnawing feelings of emptiness. Every one of my failed attempts restricts the joy that I had hoped to find and leaves me feeling trapped. Forgive me for trying to find satisfaction outside of you.

Thank you for faithfully guiding me back to the broad place. Thank you for reminding me that continual obedience leads to intimacy with you. Through faith in the work of Christ and by the power of your Holy Spirit, you enable me to live a life pleasing to you.

Thank you for setting me free from slavery to sin and the punishment of death (Rom. 8:2). Thank you for giving me the desire to obey your Word, an urging much stronger than the appetites of my flesh. Thank you for the freedom that comes in walking continually in your truth.

At every point where I am tempted, remind me that sin only confines me. Help me understand that ignoring your Word is never the path to liberty. Grant me a holy hatred of my sin and an earnest desire to keep your Word forever and ever. Strengthen my resolve to put my sin to death (Col. 3:5). May the freedom I have found in you encourage other believers to find the broad place.

Shameless

I will speak of your testimonies
before kings and not be ashamed.

—Psalm 119:46

A strange reticence threatens to choke the life out of our witness in the world. We speak confidently and without restraint on nearly any topic that interests us. With little effort, we converse fluently on subjects that we have no interest in. We are quite capable of waxing eloquent on anything, ranging from sports to politics. Not even genuine ignorance about something can restrain us from boisterously inserting our uninformed opinions. Yet we often find ourselves shamefully demure when it comes to representing God's truth to the world. The world's hostility to God's truth along with our fears of reprisal exacerbates our temptation to fall shamefully silent. May God teach us to respond to opposition like the psalmist who refused to fall silent.

How can a man who faced the cruel slander of rulers (v. 23) boldly testify before them? Courage to share God's Word with the world is a by-product of loving God's Word (vv. 47–48) and spending time in it (v. 45). No training can replace the empowering experience of spending time in God's Word on a daily basis. Those who consistently spend time in the Bible find a way to represent God's truth to others. The natural pressures that so often silence believers cannot overpower the blazing furnace from within those who regularly feast on God's Word (Jer. 20:9). Not even the most powerful can intimidate those who passionately seek God through His Word. When we spend time in the Bible, the desire to be faithful to the Lord conquers our base instincts for approval and self-preservation.

The psalmist's commitment to testify before kings is not a reckless aspiration but a calculated determination to trust the Lord. He knows that he will not "be ashamed" because God is faithful. If we shrink back from our testimony fearing shame, we will inherit the shame that God would have protected us from had we been faithful. But remember, speaking God's Word is not just an individual responsibility. We have a congregational mandate to speak God's truth before those in positions of authority. God calls His church to "contend for the faith that was once for all entrusted to God's holy people" (Jude 1:3). We must stand firm in one spirit, contending as one for the faith of the gospel (Phil. 1:7). The church must never be silent in the face of a lost and dying world. May the Lord replace our reticence with a heart that is eager to give the reason for the hope within us (1 Pet. 3:15).

Raised Hands

I delight in your commandments
because I love them.
I lift up my hands unto your commandments
which I love and I meditate on your statutes.

—Psalm 119:47–48

Father, I love your Word. Your Word gives me the opportunity to know you. Thank you for revealing to me your love, mercy, and grace through the pages of the Bible. Thank you for giving me the opportunity to study your power and might. Thank you for the wisdom that your Word gives me. Thank you for confronting my sin as I read your Word. Thank you for encouraging, comforting, and equipping me through your Word. Thank you for the hope that you fill me with as I cling to your promises. Thank you for giving me joy as I learn to walk in obedience. Thank you for giving me direction when I feel confused. Thank you for giving me strength in my weakness. Thank you for opening my eyes to your faithfulness. Thank you for teaching me about the ministry of the Holy Spirit. Thank you for revealing Jesus to me through your Word.

I confess that I sometimes give in to the temptation to delight in the things of this world. I am all too often impressed with the vanity that surrounds me. Countless times I have stood in amazement of things that pale in comparison to the beauty of your Word. Forgive me for neglecting the opportunity to stand in awe of your commandments. I have not even begun to scratch the surface of the supreme riches contained in your Word.

Father, teach me to love and delight in your commandments. Give me a committed passion for your Word. May my delight in your statutes lighten the weight of my burdens on a daily basis. Help me to invigorate my brothers and sisters in Christ in their love for the Bible. May my example elevate the importance of your Word in the hearts of my fellow believers. Tonight, I raise my hands to you in worship, thanking you for your Word.

My Comfort

Remember the word to your servant,
for I have put my hope in it.
This is my comfort in my affliction,
that your word gives me life.
The arrogant mock me exceedingly,
but I have not turned from your law.
I remember your judgments from of old, Oh Lord,
and I am comforted by them.

—Psalm 119:49–52

There is a helplessness that sweeps across me when I stare into the face of someone reeling in emotional pain. I cannot bring a widow's husband of fifty years back to life. I cannot change the fact that a woman's handicapped son was so depressed he committed suicide. I cannot fix the pain of young people living in broken families. There is certainly nothing I can do to fix a marriage filled with anger and bitterness. My heart breaks as I look into the eyes of those who have suffered as a result of sexual abuse. As a pastor, all that remains is to love them, pray for them, and walk through the valley with them. Thankfully, there is plenty that God can do in these situations to comfort.

Your God is the "Father of compassion and the God of all comfort" (2 Cor. 1:3). He will comfort you as you turn to His Word. For twenty centuries, Christians have desperately clung to God's promises in the midst of pain, loss, grief, and persecution. God's ancient Word provides more comfort than any contemporary salve this world has to offer. Most of the things we turn to for comfort only temporarily make us feel better. Whether it's shopping, eating, or browsing the Internet, most of us have something we turn to when we don't want to face our problems. All of these things serve merely to distract us from our pain.

They are completely impotent to help us face the searing pain of life. God's Word, however, gives life and comfort.

Comfort is not the absence of problems but the grace to experience life in the midst of them. Don't run from your situation. Don't ignore it either. Resist every temptation to dull the pain of your experience with the refuse of this world. Instead, turn to God's Word. All too often, our temptation in the midst of adversity is to turn from the very words that give comfort. The psalmist undoubtedly faced this temptation, but resolved not to forsake God's Word. Even while his enemies mocked him, the psalmist exclaimed, "I have not turned from your laws" (v. 51).

Find comfort as you cling to God's ancient Word today. Allow God's Word to speak life into your pain, anxiety, and tragedy. Turn to the Bible in the midst of every relational problem and financial challenge. Confront your fears by inclining your ear to God's unchanging truth. Embrace the comfort of God's Word and experience life in the midst of your hardship. As the Lord helps you, remember that He, "comforts us in all our troubles, so that we can comfort those in any trouble with the comfort we ourselves receive from God" (2 Cor. 1:4). May the comfort of Jesus Christ overflow from you to your brothers and sisters in Christ (2 Cor. 1:5).

"Comfort, comfort my people, says your God."

—Isaiah 40:1

My Song

Rage seizes me because of the wicked
who have forsaken your law.
Your statutes have been my song
in the house of my journey.
I remember in the night your name,
Oh Lord, and I will keep your law.
This is my practice; I keep your precepts.
—Psalm 119:53–56

Father, you are worthy of the loudest praise, both now and into the rest of eternity. You have no equal; there is none like you (Ps. 86:8). You are the author of my salvation (Heb. 2:10), my defender (Isa. 19:20), my strength (Ps. 27:1), and my song (Exod. 15:2).

Your Word will fuel my song until the day I stand before you in glory. My loudest songs and my faintest melodies will be about your Word. Your Word will saturate every verse, every chorus, and every refrain of my song. On my best days and on my worst days I will sing. Even in the darkest night, I will sing of your Word. No matter where I go in my journey, I will sing of your Word. Even while the world mocks me and forsakes you, I will keep singing of your Word.

Thank you for giving me joy as I journey through this life. Thank you for giving me a song to sing in the midst of my trials. Thank you for wanting to hear my frail and faltering lips sing your truth. Thank you for giving me strength to sing when it seems impossible.

I confess that I don't always want to sing. I don't feel like singing when I am disappointed, frustrated, or hurt. When I'm discouraged I find it very difficult to sing to you. Sometimes, when I'm angry, singing is the last thing that I want to do. Instead of singing, my mouth is tempted to overflow with criticism, complaints, and grumbling. Forgive me.

My voice might be plain, but my heart is desperate to sing you the most glorious chorus. Make something beautiful out of my songs. May my songs capture the attention of those who don't know you. Beckon the lost to you through my earnest songs. Help me to sing when I'm in pain just as passionately as I sing when I'm full of joy. May frustration, disappointment, and stress be fertile ground for new songs of praise as I consider your promises. Strengthen me to sing when my voice grows faint. May the voices of my fellow believers spur me on to sing with greater faithfulness. And may my songs encourage them toward greater obedience. In the morning, help me to "awaken the dawn" with songs of your Word (Ps. 108:2).

My Portion

The Lord is my portion;
I have promised to keep your word.
I have sought your face with my whole heart;
give me life according to your word.
I have considered my ways
and I have turned my feet unto your testimonies.
—Psalm 119:57–59

Our contentment in this life is so often dependent upon meeting an arbitrary list of expectations. When these expectations are not met, we can feel frustrated and confused. We expect to be healthy, so we are distraught when we face challenges with our health. We expect to have financial security, so we are unsettled when we have difficulty paying the bills. We expect to be liked, so we are shocked when people don't like us. We expect to be successful, so challenges in life confound us to the point of despair. What if your only expectation in this life was God?

When you come to faith in Jesus Christ, He becomes your grand expectation. You are not guaranteed wealth, success, or health as a believer. You are, however, guaranteed God. From the moment you first believe, you can trust that God will be your inheritance in this life and in the life to come. God will be your portion every morning. You can rely on the faithfulness of God throughout the course of every day. When you lie down each night, you can sleep peacefully, knowing that you will awaken to God's unfailing love (Ps. 90:14).

If God is your portion, seek Him with all of your heart in the Bible. Every verse, chapter, and book of the Bible provides you the opportunity to delight in your inheritance. Every moment spent in God's Word broadens your understanding of the glorious gift you have through faith in Jesus Christ. Find life as you revel in your inheritance. Consider your ways and turn your feet back to God, who is eager to give you grace, mercy, and forgiveness. Lay down unbiblical expectations in this life and seek the glorious inheritance you have through faith in the work of Jesus Christ. Look for ways to point your brothers and sisters in Christ toward their inheritance. Together, exchange your disappointment in this life with the unfathomable riches you have as a child of God.

Quickly

I will hasten and not delay to keep your commandments.
—Psalm 119:60

Father, my flesh desires to rush toward sin. I have been eager to judge, criticize, and grumble in my spirit. My flesh does not want to delay in satisfying unholy cravings. I have at times been quick to anger and quick to bitterness. I have hastily put myself first and neglected the needs of others. I have been swift to trust in myself instead of waiting on you. It does not take long for me to lose heart and become discouraged. Forgive my haste in disobeying you.

I also confess that I have been slow to obey you. I rationalize my lethargy in doing what I know to be right with countless excuses. Although I acknowledge the right thing to do, I tend to procrastinate by saying, "not yet." I console myself with my good intentions of eventually doing the right thing, but eventually I lose interest and forget. I have forfeited seeing you do great things through my listless obedience. Forgive my sloth in obeying you.

Despite my sin, you have been faithful to teach me. You have impressed your Word on my heart and mind in so many ways. You have spoken your truth to me through teachers, preachers, and friends. You have gently reminded me countless times of my need to obey. You have waited patiently for me to do the right thing.

Help me "hasten and not delay to keep your commandments."
Give me an earnest desire to do everything you have told me to do.
Keep me from the sin of postponing what I know to be your will.
Guard me from becoming distracted from even the smallest act of
obedience. When your will seems impossible, help me to take the
first step of obedience, whatever that may be. Bless each tiny step of
obedience so that I will have strength to take the next step. May your
Holy Spirit prompt me to obey you immediately. Grant me your grace
to repent quickly after your Spirit convicts me of sin. Keep me from
languishing in behavior that you have convicted me of. Help me to
walk in the joy of obeying you at the moment of your prompting.

Midnight

The cords of the wicked have bound me;
I have not forgotten your law.
In the middle of the night,
I rise to thank you for your righteous judgments.

—Psalm 119:61–62

The middle of the night is a time of turmoil and devastation in the Old Testament. In the "middle of the night," the Lord swept through the land of Egypt and killed every firstborn child and animal, a calamity that prompted "loud wailing throughout Egypt—worse than there has ever been or ever will be" (Exod. 11:4–6). This divine scourge must have indelibly impacted the Hebrew concept of "midnight" because Job 34:19–20 refers to it as the time when God sends death on the wicked. Facing intense persecution from the wicked, the psalmist describes himself as rising in the "middle of the night."

What do you do in the "middle of the night" when your mind endlessly toils over your problems? How do you respond when the darkness of your situation envelopes you, leaving you sleepless? Do you panic and lose sight of God's faithfulness? Are you tempted to blame others or lash out at God? Do you dread the morning because you know you will have to face your problems? Living underneath this stress can compromise your health and steal the joy out of every moment. It can cause you to stoop to new lows you never thought yourself capable of. Knowing the pain of such circumstances makes me marvel at how the psalmist reacted.

In the middle of the night, the psalmist rises and gives thanks for the Lord's righteous judgments. He did not rise to defend himself or to level a complaint against the Lord. He did not rise to wallow in self-pity. He did not give up on his faith or sink into the mire of despair. He did not threaten anybody or give God an ultimatum; he gave thanks. This is not simply the sheer determination of a man who had purposed to obey the Lord. It is evidence of how much the psalmist hoped in God's Word. In the midst of unrighteous persecution, he knew that he could trust in God's righteousness.

Though the middle of the night was a time of horrific judgment for the Egyptians, it was the signature of God's magnificent grace toward Israel. If you have been redeemed by the blood of the Lamb, you have an opportunity to rejoice in the "middle of the night." Trust in God's righteousness in the midst of your situation. God is infinitely just and perfect in His dealing with you. God has not forgotten about you. He is acutely aware of your situation. In fact, there is not one detail about your problem that has escaped His notice. Instead of filling your mind with how you will manage the situation, turn to the Lord and trust His righteousness. Worrying and talking incessantly about your problems will only aggravate your misery. When awakened by your problems in the middle of the night, experience the joy of complete rest in Him.

Friends

I am a companion to all who fear you,
to those who keep your precepts.
Your steadfast love fills the earth;
teach me your statutes.
—Psalm 119:63–64

Father, thank you for the gift of companionship in this difficult world. Your people are my companions through this life. In a world filled with people who do not fear you, thank you for brothers and sisters who obey your Word. Thank you for blessing me with friends who support and pray for me. Thank you that I never have to rejoice or mourn alone. Thank you for those who minister to me in my time of need. Thank you for those who hold me accountable and speak truth into my life. Thank you for the opportunity to witness your grace lived out in those around me and for the ways that their example challenges me. Your people and your church are my companions.

But I confess that I have not always cared to involve myself with your church. At times I have acted on worldly feelings of independence and self-reliance. In an attempt to insulate myself from the problems of others, I have neglected the people you died to redeem. I confess that I have not always returned acts of kindness with the same measure of love and concern. I have arrogantly treated my personal time as more important than the privilege of worshipping with my brothers and sisters in Christ. I have passed up many opportunities to disciple and equip younger believers with the wonderful truths that you have taught me. Sometimes I have responded harshly to those within your church who disappointed me.

Help me to experience the love you have filled this earth with as I love my brothers and sisters in Christ. Help me seize opportunities to minister to them. Give me strength to serve your people. No servant should be above his master. You washed your disciples' feet; help me to wash the feet of my fellow believers (John 13:14–17). Guard me from the sin of indifference toward your people. Teach me to be gracious, loving, and kind. As I consider the ways in which you have extended mercy to me, help me to freely forgive those who wrong me. Open my eyes to the blessing of serving those you died to redeem.

Affliction

*You have done good with your servant,
according to your word, Oh Lord.*
*Teach me knowledge and good judgment,
for I believe in your commandments.*
Before I was afflicted I strayed, but now I keep your word.
You are good and do good; teach me your statutes.
*The arrogant have forged lies against me,
but I will keep your precepts with all of my heart.*
Their heart is unfeeling as fat, but I delight in your law.
It was good for me that I was afflicted so that I might learn your statutes.
—Psalm 119:65–71

We are well acquainted with the misery of affliction, but how often do we consider the blessings of it? Affliction cannot extinguish the eternal goodness of God. God is infinitely good in the midst of every storm in life. One of the ways God demonstrates His goodness in the midst of your problems is by teaching you. There are many lessons that you can learn during any season in life, but some you will never learn unless you face affliction. What might God teach you in the midst of your trial?

The psalmist prayed, "Before I was afflicted I strayed, but now I keep your word" (v. 69). Enduring the relentless attacks of the wicked helped him cultivate an obedient life. God wants you to learn obedience in the midst of your suffering. Even the Lord Jesus "learned obedience from what he suffered" (Heb. 5:8). If suffering was important to the Lord Jesus, surely we would not think that we can skip this step. Ease and comfort do not always stimulate radical obedience. During times of relative ease, a lethargic complacency so often creeps in. In addition to obedience, God also wants to teach you about His Word in the midst of your problems.

The psalmist exclaims, "It was good for me that I was afflicted so that I might learn your statutes" (v. 71). Suffering produces an acute focus on the Lord that almost nothing else in life can. You can blame the Lord for allowing hardship or you can bless Him for wanting to teach you (Heb. 12:6). Your understanding of God's Word will remain adolescent if you do not seek God through His Word in the midst of suffering. Suffering is an ideal time to study God's Word. Imagine all of the incredible things that God is waiting to teach you!

Today, you get to choose what your focus will be. Will you respond to your problems with frustration or will you leverage them to draw near to Jesus Christ? Will you lash out in anger or will you beg God to teach you obedience? Do not let the pain of affliction blind you from experiencing the incredible blessings available to you. Choose not to squander your hardship. Determine to seek God through His Word in the midst of it. Draw near to Christ and experience victory. Humbly learn everything God wants you to learn in the midst of your trials. With this knowledge, minister to your brothers and sisters in Christ who are languishing under their affliction. As you draw near to God, you will see the goodness of God and be able to exclaim along with the psalmist, "You have been good to me."

Better than Gold

*The law from your mouth is better to me
than thousands of pieces of gold and silver.*
—Psalm 119:72

Father, nothing in this world compares to the magnificence of your Word. Thousands of pieces of silver and gold will never approximate the limitless worth of your perfect Word. Thank you for granting me full and unfettered access to such a marvelous treasure.

Nothing in this world can give me peace, hope, or joy like your promises. No amount of money could ever purchase my salvation. No accumulation of worldly possessions could ever delight my soul. Living for the things of this world robs me of the peace that you made available through Christ. Far from benefitting me, I find that the things of this world distract, trouble, and disappoint me. Without you, everything in this world is profoundly vain (Eccles. 1:3).

I confess the sin of treating the things of this world as though they compare to the supreme excellence of your Word. Though not with my mouth, my actions sometimes reveal that I place more value on the perishing things of this world rather than on your eternal truth. Countless times, I have set your Word aside to pursue vanity. I have been zealous for money at times yet cold toward your Word. I have given tacit approval to the emptiness of this world by purchasing things I don't need while at the same time ignoring opportunities to indulge in the Bible. As stuff accumulates around my house, I find myself increasingly in want for the things of God.

Teach me to store up treasures in heaven "where moth and vermin do not destroy, and where thieves do not break in and steal" (Matt. 6:20). May the "deceitfulness of wealth" never choke out the power of your Word in my life; may it always be fruitful (Mark 4:19). Help me live "free from the love of money" and to be content with what you have given me (Heb. 13:5). Since the "love of money is a root of all kinds of evil" (1 Tim. 6:10), help me to "pursue righteousness, godliness, faith, love, endurance and gentleness" as I study your Word (1 Tim. 6:11).

Teach me to be more like Moses, who "regarded disgrace for the sake of Christ as of greater value than the treasures of Egypt" (Heb. 11:26). Conform me to the image of your Son who spurned a life of wealth so that He could enrich others (2 Cor. 8:9). May my life encourage other saints to value your Word above any earthly treasure.

His Hands

Your hands made me and formed me;
give me understanding
and I will learn your commandments.

—Psalm 119:73

You are not the product of some complex biological process. God knew you and loved you before you were born. With His hands, He made you just the way He wanted you to be (Ps. 139:13–16). Since God is powerful and intimately acquainted with every aspect of your being, He is perfectly suited to teach you His commandments. The God who created your mind with His powerful hand can open it to receive His perfect truth.

The psalmist does not appeal to God's power for wealth, success, victory, money, or possessions, but for understanding in God's Word. Why in the world would the psalmist appeal to the Creator of the Universe for something so seemingly insignificant? Oh, but there is nothing insignificant about understanding God's Word.

Understanding and obeying God's Word changes everything about us. Comprehending God's eternal truth makes us courageous. David did not slay Goliath by his might but by understanding God's Word. With defiance, David spoke to the giant, saying, "You come against me with sword and spear and javelin, but I come against you in the name of the LORD Almighty, the God of the armies of Israel ..." (1 Sam. 17:45). David's confidence in the promise of the Lord's presence gave him all of the courage he needed to say, "This day the LORD will deliver you into my hands, and I'll strike you down and cut off your head ..." (1 Sam. 17:46). But this is not simply an individualistic pursuit. As churches understand God's Word and obey it, God changes entire families, neighborhoods, and communities—indeed, the world! Understanding God's Word is not a luxury for the people of God. Ignorance of God's Word leads to destruction. Isaiah prophesied, "my people will go into exile for lack of understanding; those of high rank will die of hunger and the common people will be parched with thirst. Therefore Death expands its jaws, opening wide its mouth; into it will descend their nobles and masses with all their brawlers and revelers" (Isa. 5:13–14). The smallest shred of biblical understanding will always outperform passion, zeal, and education.

Ask the God who created the universe to give you understanding in His Word. Cry out to the God who made you for a deeper comprehension of the Bible. Ask Him to give you understanding, then believe and obey everything He teaches you. Labor to bring your fellow believers into an understanding of God's Word. May the very hands that fashioned us open our minds to understand His commandments.

A Beautiful Sight

May those who fear you, see me and rejoice
because I have put my hope in your word.

—Psalm 119:74

Father, tonight I thank you for the joy I have in being part of your church. Thank you for all of the strength and encouragement I draw from your people. Thank you for all of the laughter and fellowship that I have enjoyed. Thank you for all of the precious memories I have through the years of spending time with your people. Thank you that I am not alone.

Help me be the kind of Christian that prompts rejoicing in the hearts of other believers. Without a devotion to your Word, I will never be a catalyst for joy in the hearts of my brothers and sisters in Christ. So grant me a greater commitment to your Word. May my relentless hope in your Word ignite rejoicing within your church. For the sake of my fellow believers, guard me from the sin of disregarding your Word.

But I have not always been the source of joy amidst your people. At times, I have stifled their joy. I confess that I have been the source of needless angst in the hearts of my fellow believers. I am also guilty of busying myself to the point where no time remains to be concerned for the countenance of my brothers and sisters in Christ. Forgive me for being aloof toward those you died to redeem. Instead of prompting joy, I have fueled frustration and division over mere preferences. In my heart, I have criticized and judged your people instead of praying for them. I have not always been quick to forgive. At other times, I have been so consumed with concern for myself that I have not even bothered to care whether or not my life brought joy to other believers. Forgive me for my indifference.

Cause my love for your people to overflow (1 Thess. 3:12). Help me encourage them and build them up in the Lord (1 Thess. 5:11). Help me to be relentlessly patient and kind to everybody, never keeping a record of wrongs (1 Cor. 13:4–5). May my hope in your Word prompt others to rejoice and hope in your Word. Fill your church with joy as we seek Christ in your Word.

Love

*I know, Oh Lord, that your judgments are righteous,
and in faithfulness you have afflicted me.*

*May your steadfast love comfort me,
according to your word to your servant.*

*May your compassion come to me and I will live,
for your law is my delight.*

—Psalm 119:75–77

Your hardship is not evidence that God has turned away from you, but a reminder that He loves you. God disciplines those He loves (Heb. 12:6). The psalmist even went so far as to say, "in faithfulness, you have afflicted me." Far from being absent in our suffering, your heavenly Father is Lord over every aspect of it. God is sovereign and faithful in the midst of your turmoil. He is our "ever-present help in trouble" (Ps. 46:1). Sometimes the help does not come in the form of removing your affliction. In torment, Paul prayed desperately for his thorn in the flesh to be taken away, but instead of removing it, the Lord said, "My grace is sufficient for you, for my power is made perfect in weakness" (2 Cor. 12:7–9). Whether or not God delivers you from hardship, know that God still loves you.

Your God is rich in love (Ps. 145:8). He is "compassionate and gracious, slow to anger, abounding in love" (Ps. 103:8). He "longs to be gracious to you; … he will rise up to show you compassion …" (Isa. 30:18). He loved you so much He gave His only Son to die on a cross (John 3:16). There is no greater love than the glorious love displayed on the cross (John 15:13). God's love is powerful and enduring. "We are more than conquerors through him who loved us" (Rom. 8:37). Nothing "in all creation, will be able to separate us from the love of God that is in Christ Jesus our Lord" (Rom. 8:39). God's love is always enough!

God loves you when you fail just as much as He loves you when you succeed. He loves you when you are poor just like He loves you when you have plenty. He loves you in the midst of your sorrow the same as He loves you when you are happy. He loves you when you feel all alone and when you are surrounded by great friends. He loves you when you are tired, irritated, and frustrated just like He loves you when you are at your best. God's love is enough in the midst of your fear and anxiety. It is enough during your seasons of grief and mourning. Should you face unthinkable tragedy, His love is enough. God's love is also enough when you have exhausted all of your energy and strength. Do not question God's love when you face trials. Instead, lean into Him with all of your might and experience His torrential love!

Falsely Accused

May the arrogant be ashamed, for they have wronged me falsely;
I will meditate on your precepts.
May those who fear you turn to me,
those who know your testimonies.
May my heart be blameless in your statutes
so that I will not be ashamed.

—Psalm 119:78–80

Father, thank you for dealing with those who have wronged me. Thank you, Lord, that I do not bear the responsibility of repaying the arrogant for their evil. Vengeance belongs to you and you will repay (Rom. 12:19). I trust that you will put the arrogant to shame in your perfect timing. To respond to their folly with folly of my own would make me like them (Prov. 26:4–5); instead, I will meditate on your precepts.

In turning to your Word, help me find the companionship of those who fear you. Help me become a harbor for believers who face false accusations. May the wounded and hurting seek me out. Encourage your saints through my example.

I confess that I have reacted to the arrogant with arrogance of my own. I have given in to the temptation to repay evil for evil (1 Pet. 3:9). During times in which I succeeded in remaining silent, my angry thoughts condemned me before you, the God who knows my heart (Acts 15:8).

Teach me to turn the other cheek (Matt. 5:39) and to return evil with blessings (1 Pet. 3:9). Keep me from being reckless with my words (Prov. 12:18). Grant me your grace as I seek to "overcome evil with good" (Rom. 12:21). Help me love my enemies and pray for those who persecute me (Matt. 5:44). Guard me from the same sins that will bring shame and judgment on the arrogant. Thank you for giving me the righteousness of your Son, Jesus Christ. Help me to pursue a blameless life by the power of the Holy Spirit. Tonight, I rest knowing that you are able to keep me from falling, and to present me before your "glorious presence without fault and with great joy" (Jude 1:24).

Gloriously Faint

My soul languishes for your salvation;
I hope in your word.
My eyes fail for your words,
saying, "when will you comfort me?"
—Psalm 119:81–82

What could drive a man to search God's Word to the point of visual impairment? The question is probably moot for most self-professing Christians whose time in God's Word can only be characterized as sporadic and careless. The aloof engagement that most Christians have with Scripture keeps them free from any inconvenient entanglements with God's truth. Though God's Word is "useful for teaching, rebuking, correcting and training in righteousness" (2 Tim. 3:16), many believers are content with their superficial devotionals that contain nothing more than inspirational thoughts to start the day. In the same perfunctory manner that many might sip their morning coffee, a small percentage of Christians casually read a verse or two. But desperate searching, digging, and studying are abnormal for believers in the twenty-first century. Sadly, Christians reserve their eyes for more mindless activities like watching television, surfing the Internet, and staring at their phones. Video games and gossip periodicals have become equally captivating to millions of Christian people. None of us are immune to these temptations.

In contrast to the status quo, a small minority of believers employ their eyes to pore over the Scripture for divine comfort. They feverishly search, study, and feast on His Word—not to accumulate knowledge but to draw near to their Savior. The Word of God represents their life, their strength, and their hope. Their hope is so securely fastened on the Lord that the thought of trusting in anything else seems absurd. As a result, their eyes grow gloriously faint from their powerful hope in Christ.

Have you yet reached the conclusion that you are absolutely desperate for the Lord? On good days and on bad days alike, you are desperate for God. For the rest of eternity, you will never experience a single moment when you do not need the Lord Jesus Christ. Your hardships are a blessed reminder of this simple fact and should drive you relentlessly into the Word of God for hope and comfort. Resist the temptation to languish over the superficial things of this world. Instead, feed voraciously on the Scripture for comfort. Fix your eyes on Jesus, the author and perfecter of your faith (Heb. 12:2). Search the Bible for God's promises and hang every hope on them. With weary eyes, devour God's Word until your heart finds the peace that "transcends all understanding" (Phil. 4:7).

In the Smoke

For I have been like a wineskin in the smoke;
I have not forgotten your statutes.
—Psalm 119:83

Father, you are worthy of my best attempts to seek you, even when I am suffering. Your infinite greatness and my helplessness demand that I seek you in the midst of the greatest tribulation. Even when I feel as though I am being roasted slowly over a fire, you deserve my devotion.

I confess that this kind of obedience seems unachievable since I so often fail to obey when times are easy. My flesh resists discomfort on nearly every level. I confess that I don't want to be inconvenienced most of the time. Forgive me for my selfish unwillingness to seek you through your Word when I am going through difficulty. I confess that while I am easily distracted from reading your Word, I somehow manage to give my undivided attention to a host of things that do not matter. Forgive me for my vanity.

Lord, you forgive my sin, heal my diseases, redeem my life from the pit, and satisfy my desires with good things—help me not to forget all your benefits (Ps. 103:2–5). In the best of times and the worst of times, give me an inexhaustible commitment to your Word. Remove from me every vestige of slothfulness that might hinder a faithful pursuit of you during suffering. Eliminate every trace of pride that might persuade me to think that I am capable of handling difficulties on my own. May the searing heat of suffering give me a greater awareness of my desperation for you.

Keep the challenges of my life from becoming a wedge that drives me away from you. Instead, may every problem and hardship drive me closer to you. I know that I am not alone when I walk through the fire (Isa. 43:2). Sustain me by your Word when I am in the smoke. Guard me from fear and captivate me with the beauty of your Word. In the crucible of my suffering, galvanize within me a greater thirst for Jesus Christ.

Facing Death

How long are the days of your servant?
When will you execute judgment on those who persecute me?
The arrogant dig pits for me, which are not in keeping with your law.
All of your commandments are faithful; they persecute me falsely—help me.
They almost destroyed me on the earth,
but I have not forsaken your precepts.
—Psalm 119:84–87

Have you ever been in a situation where you thought you might not make it out alive? The fear of death can incapacitate people and drive them past the point of despair. It can make you sick or spark extraordinary heroism and bravery. Our instinctual terror in near-death experiences illustrates our potent desire to live. Like the urge to eat and drink, we all share the strong impulse to survive. The innate desire to survive makes every other need pale in comparison. However, followers of Christ must have an even stronger determination to obey God's Word.

Though persecuted within inches of his life, the psalmist demonstrated an impenetrable commitment to God's Word. He chose the possibility of death over rebellion against God. When put to the test, his determination to obey God's Word was stronger than his desire to live. One thing is clear: you are living in a day that will test your faith.

The Scripture prophesies that during the last days, Christians will be "handed over to be persecuted and put to death" (Matt. 24:9). In response to the suffering, "many will turn away from the faith" (Matt. 24:10). These are the very same people who will take the mark of the beast simply so that they can continue commerce (Rev. 13:16). In short, many will choose survival over fidelity to the Lord in the last days. But Jesus says, "the one who stands firm to the end will be saved" (Mark 13:13).

Standing in stark contrast to those who will fall away, we have the courageous example of believers who withstood inexpressible suffering. The author of Hebrews records, "Some faced jeers and flogging, and even chains and imprisonment. They were put to death by stoning; they were sawed in two; they were killed by the sword. They went about in sheepskins and goatskins, destitute, persecuted and mistreated—the world was not worthy of them" (Heb. 11:36–38). What about you? Would you rather forsake God's Word and "live" or remain faithful to the Lord and die? "We do not belong to those who shrink back and are destroyed, but to those who have faith and are saved" (Heb. 10:39). You do not get to choose when you will die, but you do have a choice as to how you will live. Live with a reckless commitment to God's Word. Honor the Lord Jesus in life. Honor the Lord Jesus in death.

Live to Obey

According to your steadfast love,
give me life and I will keep the testimonies of your mouth.
—Psalm 119:88

Father, I thank you for your steadfast love – the love that brings life. Though I could never repay you, I will live the rest of my life in careful obedience to your words: words that come from your mouth. Your Word is not a repository of sterile, religious truisms, but words spoken by you—words filled with life and power, words that convey your eternal love and perfect compassion, words that surprise and overwhelm me, words that confront my sin and comfort my heart, words that give me hope and encouragement, words that reveal your Son Jesus to me. Thank you for the words from your mouth.

I don't want to live my life chasing the unsatisfying vanities of the world. Nor do I wish to indulge my fleshly appetites with things that leave me famished and empty. A life void of obedience to you is a life wasted. As you give me life, I will give you obedience.

My commitment to obey your Word is not a cheap promise, but the earnest desire of my heart. I commit myself to obeying your Word, not because I think I can do it, but because the work of Christ has made obedience possible. I commit myself to obeying you because through Christ Jesus, the Holy Spirit has set me free from slavery to sin (Rom. 8:2). Your Spirit that raised Jesus from the grave lives in me and empowers me to live a life that honors you (Rom. 8:11).

Nevertheless, I know that I will fail from time to time in my pursuit of obedience to your Word. You alone know the full scope of my failures. Even now, I confess the ways in which you have found my obedience wanting today. But my failures don't keep me from committing myself fully to your Word. Instead, my sin reminds me of your grace made possible through your Son's death and resurrection —a grace I receive by faith, a grace that enables me to run after you, knowing that all of my failures are covered. I rest in this grace tonight and trust that it will propel me to new heights of obedience tomorrow.

In the Heavens

Forever, Oh Lord, your word is stationed in the heavens.
Your faithfulness continues from generation to generation;
you established the earth and it stands firm.
Your judgments stand today,
for all of them are your servants.

—Psalm 119:89–91

Have you ever scribbled words onto a beach only to see the waves effortlessly dissolve them? In the same way, most things in this life will come and go. Cultural trends that are "all the rage" will eventually appear old and antiquated to younger generations who will naively think their "new" ways have never been tried before. From fashions to technology, most things in life will come and go with the same predictability. Even well-respected teachings and philosophies will gradually seem useless. Proponents of these philosophies will rise to prominence then, one by one, die in obscurity, receiving only footnotes in the ever-growing volume of literature. To compensate for this deficiency, there will be a seemingly endless creation of books (Eccles. 12:12), books that will eventually be ignored and thrown away. Unlike nearly everything else in life, the Word of God remains forever.

Just as God created the heavenly bodies and fixed them in their places, God stationed His Word in the heavens. As the heavens endure, the Word of God endures. His Word remains the same because it reflects the character of God who never changes (Mal. 3:6; Heb. 13:8). God's "faithfulness continues from generation to generation." God's Word will never need revisions, retractions, corrections, or updates. In contrast to the growing list of irrelevant books that will be disregarded, God's Holy book stands firm.

After many centuries, God's Word still encourages you, still comforts you, and still gives you hope. The Bible still provides the message of salvation and the hope of heaven. God's Word still gives you direction and teaches you how to live a life that honors God. The Bible still reveals Jesus Christ and trains you in righteousness. God's Word still strengthens you. The Bible still teaches you how to worship, pray, and serve your brothers and sisters in Christ. God's Word is stationed in the heavens. Give yourself fully to the study of God's Word today! Thank Him for giving you such a lasting and wonderful gift.

If Not

If your law had not been my delight,
then I would have perished in my affliction.
—Psalm 119:92

Father, I thank you for teaching me to delight in your Word. Through delighting in your Word, you have ransomed my life from an empty, meaningless existence.

If not for your Word, I would have crumbled underneath the pressures of life. Delighting in your Word gave me a bold resolve to face otherwise debilitating problems.

If not for your Word, I would have persisted in my sin. I would not have turned from the things that grieve you without your Word.

If not for your Word, I would have followed my vain pursuits. I would still be zealously pursuing my own agenda if not for your Word.

If not for your Word, I would have never discovered your calling on my life. Your Word helped me completely surrender my life to following your will.

If not for your Word, I would have never experienced the abundant life that you promise. As I have delighted in your Word, you have taught me the joy of my salvation.

If not for your Word, I would have never experienced the assurance of my salvation. I would be living in anxiety and doubt today without your Word.

If not for your Word, I would not love my brothers and sisters in Jesus Christ. Long ago, I would have determined that I could live the Christian life on my own.

If not for your Word, I would have never forgiven those who have hurt me. I would be suffering in the mire of bitterness without your Word.

If not for your Word, I would not know your Son Jesus the way I do. Your Word reveals the person and work of Jesus so that I can know Him, love Him, and serve Him.

If not for your Word, I would not know how to worship. Your Word teaches me how to pray, rejoice, praise, and exalt in Jesus Christ.

I Am Yours

Forever, I will not forget your precepts,
for by them you have given me life.
I am yours;
save me, for I have sought your precepts.
The wicked wait to destroy me;
I will consider your testimonies.

—Psalm 119:93–95

With his life on the line, the psalmist exclaims in desperation, "I am yours." Belonging to the Lord is the most compelling reason he can give for his request. As a child would cry out for his father's help, the psalmist is saying, "I am your Son, you are my Father, help me—I have no one else to turn to." No father who understands his responsibility to protect and provide can ignore the helpless cry of his child. But many with absolutely no connection with the Lord say the same. Even today, the refrain, "We are all God's children" continues to be popularized by people with no earthly idea of what it means to be adopted as God's child through faith in Jesus Christ. Though everybody is God's creation, not everybody is God's child.

As if to establish the legitimacy of his claim, the psalmist concludes verse 94 in saying, "for I have sought your precepts." Few things in this world positively demonstrate genuine faith like spending time with the Lord in His Word. Though childlike faith might very well exist in those who have not yet started their active pursuit of God's Word, it is difficult to know for sure. Just as earthly children listen to their fathers, children of God want to hear the voice of their heavenly Father. We become sons of God through faith in Jesus (Gal. 3:26), and we demonstrate our faith, in part, by seeking to know God through His Word. Jesus said, "My sheep listen to my voice; I know them, and they follow me" (John 10:27). The force of the psalmist's plea comes not from his claim to be God's child but in how he lives out the claim.

Demonstrate the reality of your relationship with God by seeking Christ through the Word today. Today, raise your voice to God with your loudest cry, "I am yours—help me," knowing that He will not despise your plea (Ps. 102:17). Take confidence that "the prayer of the upright" always pleases the Lord (Prov. 15:8). Your heavenly Father "knows what you need before you ask him" (Matt. 6:8).

Limitless

To all perfection I have seen an end,
but your commandments are exceedingly broad.
—Psalm 119:96

Father, nothing in this world is perfect! The things that appear to be flawless eventually reveal their imperfections. Over time, even minor blemishes deepen and intensify in ways that irreversibly tarnish the original beauty. Nothing in our world is exempt from the corrosion of this fallen world. Everything in your creation groans underneath the bondage of decay caused by sin (Rom. 8:19–21). Moths silently demolish the most durable things this world has to offer (Matt. 6:19–20).

Yet, I confess that I embody the imperfection because I consistently find myself pining after the things of this world. I confess my sinful desires for the things of this world. I repent from my need to have things I do not need. Help me see the emptiness of the things my flesh longs for. I know that "No one can serve two masters. Either you will hate the one and love the other, or you will be devoted to the one and despise the other" (Matt. 6:24). I choose you. Help me long for the "inheritance that can never perish, spoil or fade" (1 Pet. 1:4).

Unlike the things of this world, your Word is infinitely perfect. If given the rest of eternity, I could never exhaust the riches of even a single verse. Your Word has no defects, no flaws, and no blemishes.

Your Word is also perfect in its completion; it contains everything that I need to know. The fullness of your Word leads me to Christ, the hope of glory (Col. 1:25–27).

Teach me to explore the limitless perfection of your Word. When I am tempted to ignore your commands, remind me of their infinite perfection. Recall to my mind how flawless your Word is when obedience seems difficult. May my actions never communicate to a lost world that your Word is lacking in some manner. Instead, help my obedience reflect the supreme worth of your Word. Help me invigorate my fellow believers to gaze upon your perfect Word.

Surpassing Wisdom

Oh how I love your law;
I meditate on it all of the day.
Your commandments make me wiser than my enemies,
for they are forever with me.
I have more insight than all my teachers,
for I meditate on your statutes.
I have more understanding than the elders,
because I have kept your precepts.
—Psalm 119:97–100

How would you respond if the Lord appeared to you in a dream and said, "Ask for whatever you want me to give you" (1 Kings 3:5)? Would you ask for wisdom like King Solomon did, or would you crave something else? Though I have no confidence in my flesh, I would love to think that I would plead for wisdom, because I know the blessings that accompany godly wisdom. I know that wisdom is more valuable than silver or gold (Prov. 3:14–15). I know that "wisdom is supreme" and that Proverbs 4:7 admonishes me to acquire it, even if it costs everything I have. I am also captivated with the promise that wisdom makes me "more powerful than ten rulers in a city" (Eccles. 7:19). If you long to know the blessings of godly wisdom, pay careful attention to how the psalmist achieved it in Psalm 119:97–100.

Love for God's Word will increase your wisdom and understanding far beyond anything else in life. The most sophisticated intellectual and educational pursuits will never enrich you in the ways that God's Word will. No measure of academic acumen will achieve for you the depth of understanding found in God's Word. In the same way, your experience will yield nothing if you do not discipline it with God's Word. When compared with the unsearchable riches of God's Word, the vast knowledge of the world's most brilliant philosophers proves foolish (1 Cor. 1:20). That's because "all the treasures of wisdom and knowledge" are hidden in Christ (Col. 2:3).

But remember, it is not simply the knowledge of God's Word that will enrich your wisdom and understanding; it's the love of it. When you love God's Word, you will immerse yourself in it and obey it with all of your heart. On the other hand, if you merely accumulate biblical knowledge, you will have achieved something vain. After all, "knowledge puffs up while love builds up" (1 Cor. 8:1). In fact, you will never truly know a biblical principle until you have lived according to it. Like a polished hammer lying unused in a toolbox, your knowledge of God's Word will profit you nothing. As James writes, "Do not merely listen to the word, and so deceive yourselves. Do what it says" (James 1:22). As you increase in knowledge, increase in obedience.

It's not surprising to learn that the psalmist had much greater wisdom than his enemies. But it is striking that his love for God's Word gave him more understanding than the elders of the land. You would assume that Israel's elders had the requisite wisdom to accompany their significant responsibility. After all, God expected them to teach Israel to obey God's Word (Deut. 27:1). Yet like so many who hold significant positions of ministry today, the elders were not zealous in their obedience to God's Word (Lam. 1:19). Consequently, their understanding paled in comparison with the psalmist's. Religious achievements will never fix a deficiency in your love for God's Word. Every opportunity to serve the Lord is an invitation from God to rely more on His Word. Love those you serve by loving God's Word.

My Teacher

I have withheld my feet from every evil path
so that I might keep your word.
I have not turned away from your judgments,
for you have taught me.
—Psalm 119:101–102

Father, I have longed to travel on paths that you have forbidden. Sometimes, a short jaunt down the wrong path seems harmless. But I restrain my feet from "every evil path so that I might keep your word." Evil paths take me to places that inflame the lust of my flesh. Sin always cultivates a desire within me for more sin. The more I sin, the less I remember the amazing fellowship that I enjoyed during seasons of obedience. So I withhold my feet from the countless evil paths "that I might keep your word."

You are the Creator of the Universe; "you give life to everything and the multitudes of heaven worship you" (Neh. 9:6). With your infinite strength, you depose rulers and overthrow nations (Hag. 2:22). You are "enthroned as King forever" (Ps. 29:10). Not one plan of yours will be thwarted (Job 42:2). You have defeated death through the resurrection of Jesus Christ (1 Cor. 15) and redeemed a representation of every nation, tribe, people and language (Rev. 7:9). "As the heavens are higher than the earth," so your ways and your thoughts are higher than mine (Isa. 55:9). No man has ever comprehended your mind or been your counselor (Rom. 11:34). Lord, there is "none like you" (Ps. 86:8).

And with your incomprehensible power and wisdom, you have taught me (Ps. 16:7). Through your Holy Spirit, you have patiently taught me your Word (John 14:26). You have met me on cold, dark mornings when I could barely keep my eyes open. You have taught me in the midst of painful trials and glorious victories. You have been patient with me when I was slow to learn. You are exalted in power; there is no teacher like you (Job 36:22). The thought of squandering your loving instruction pains me. Help me not turn from your judgments, "for you have taught me."

Like Honey

How sweet are your words to my taste,
more than honey to my mouth.
—Psalm 119:103

Have you tasted God's Word? God wants to take you far beyond simply reading and listening to the Bible. Familiarity with God's Word is never the goal. Even Satan was conversant enough with the Scripture to hurl it deceitfully at Jesus during His temptation (Matt. 4:1–10). How many people in hell today can recite well-known Scriptures and explain basic doctrines of the Church? God is calling you to the more significant task of feasting on His Word.

If you choose to "eat" God's Word, you will do everything you can to internalize it. Studying, memorizing, and meditating on God's Word will replace the more passive task of reading. With a pen and paper in hand, you will pore over the Scriptures, waiting for God to reveal Himself to you. You will meticulously investigate the elusive verses that you were formerly content to gloss mindlessly over.

As you internalize God's Word, you will discover just how sweet it is (Prov. 24:13). What could be sweeter than the incredible riches of God's grace and love for you expressed through the cross? The more you indulge in God's Word, the sweeter it becomes. Though the things of this world quickly reveal just how bitter and unsatisfying they are (Prov. 5:3–4), the Bible provides a continual banquet. This magnificent banquet does not cost you a thing. God beckons humanity, saying, "you who have no money, come, buy and eat! Come buy wine and milk without money and without cost … and eat what is good, and you will delight in the richest of fare" (Isa. 55:1–2).

Sink your teeth into God's Word. Like Ezekiel, who ate the Lord's scroll and courageously prophesied God's message of judgment to Israel (Ezek. 3:1–4). Or, like John, who ate the "little scroll" and uttered the mysteries of the apocalypse (Rev. 10:9–10). Nourished with the richest of fare, you will have great strength to share God's Word with others. Do not impoverish your service to Christ with a nominal commitment to His Word. "Taste and see that the LORD is good" (Ps. 34:8).

Godly Hatred

I get understanding from your precepts;
therefore, I hate every false path.
—Psalm 119:104

Father, thank you for giving me understanding from your precepts. Thank you for using your Word to expose the deceitfulness of "every false path." Because of your Word, I do not have to be deceived by the attractiveness of sin.

I now understand the darkness and loneliness hiding behind every alluring temptation.

I now understand the painful consequences of that which promises "satisfaction."

I now understand how sin will hurt those I love the very most.

I now understand that my sin caused you great suffering.

I now understand that sin brings shame, not freedom.

I now understand how my sin wounds your church.

I now understand that sin leads to death (Rom. 6:23).

I now understand that Satan comes to steal, kill, and destroy (John 10:10).

I now understand that my sin can lead others astray.

I now understand that sin grieves your Holy Spirit (Eph. 4:30).

I now understand that sin robs me of the joy of my salvation (Ps. 51).

I now understand that God disciplines those who engage in sin.
I now understand the emptiness of "every false path."

Father, continue to teach me your Word so that I can see the error of every rebellious way. As I grow in understanding, teach me to hate "every false path." Help me abhor every path that threatens the intimacy I have with you through your Word. Guard me from the sin of judging those traveling on "false paths." Help me to love them, but hate the wickedness they've embraced. Draw me continually toward the "path of life" and "fill me with joy in your presence, with eternal pleasures at your right hand" (Ps. 16:11).

Light

*Your word is a lamp to my feet
and a light for my path.
I have taken an oath and confirmed it,
to keep your righteous judgments.*
—Psalm 119:105–106

You will live in constant frustration if you treat God's Word like a personal flashlight that you wield in order to expedite your journey down whatever path you might choose for yourself. This verse is about the light of God's Word, not your quest to find your personal path in life. The context of Psalm 119 allows for no other conclusion; God's Word reveals the path that every Christian must travel. God is the one who shines the light of His Word, and he always shines it in the same direction: the direction of truth (John 17:17). Your job is to make your path subservient to the light, not the other way around. Do not turn to God's Word only as a means of achieving your personal ambition. Instead, make it your personal ambition to walk in God's Word.

Thankfully, the path is well-lit. But, to say that the path of God's Word is well-lit does not mean that it is an easy path. You will face great temptation to ignore the illuminated path of God's Word and follow one of the many false paths in life. False pathways will regularly appear easier and more satisfying. Those living in darkness will invariably try to beguile you with the vain promise of thrills and excitement. You may also face discouragement and fear.

By the power of the Holy Spirit, live your life walking in the light of God's Word. No matter how challenging the path of truth is, "do not turn aside to the right or to the left. Walk in obedience to all that the LORD your God has commanded you, so that you may live and prosper ..." (Deut. 5:32–33). Hang your hope on the promise that "the path of the righteous is like the morning sun, shining ever brighter till the full light of day" (Prov. 4:18). Get rid of every sinful entanglement and "run with perseverance the race marked" out for you (Heb.12:1). Stay on the well-lit path knowing that it will always lead you to Jesus, "the light of the world" (John 8:12).

Day 23 — Evening

Willing Offering

I am exceedingly afflicted, Oh Lord,
give me life according to your word.
Accept, Oh Lord, the willing offering of my mouth
and teach me your judgments.
—Psalm 119:107–108

Father, only you know the affliction I have faced. But I bring my offering of praise to you tonight because you have given me life through Jesus Christ. Through Christ, you make my heart "willing" even in the midst of trials. I know that my "present sufferings are not worth comparing with the glory that will be revealed in us" (Rom. 8:18). I also know that you are good even in the midst of my problems. You have taught me to run to you and not away from you in suffering.

Even still, I confess that I have not always responded to hardship the right way. I confess that I have been angry and bitter toward you and others. While feeling sorry for myself, I have withheld from you the "willing offerings" that you deserve. I have spent more time complaining than I have in prayer. Shamefully, I have accused you of not seeing or caring about my problems. I have even blamed you for not intervening to save me from the difficulties. All the while, I have been slow to recognize my own sin.

May the darkness of my circumstances enable me to see the brightness of your promises. Teach me to rejoice in the promise of eternal life in the midst of hardship. Prompt me by your Holy Spirit to sing loudly when I'm hurting. Overwhelm my anxiety with heartfelt praise for you. Help me awake "morning after morning" ready to bring you willing offerings (Exod. 36:3). Guard me from focusing on myself when I'm hurting. Lead me into the fellowship of believers so that I can join their chorus of praise. Be pleased with my willing worship, Oh Lord. "My heart, O God, is steadfast, my heart is steadfast; I will sing and make music" (Ps. 57:7).

Snare

My life is in my hands continually,
but I have not forgotten your law.
The wicked have set a snare for me,
but I do not stray from your precepts.
—Psalm 119:109–110

Following Christ through His Word has never been—nor will it ever be—the path of least resistance. For centuries, followers of Christ have suffered underneath the cruelty of wicked men. To obey God's Word is "to take your life into your hands." The wicked will hate you for your fidelity to God's Word, and some will lay snares (Pss. 141:9, 142:3; Jer. 18:22). But snares only work if you know with certainty where your prey will be.

There is a degree of predictability about those who obey God's Word. The wicked men in Daniel's day knew they would find Daniel on his knees (Dan. 6:5–11). Sanballat, Tobiah, and Geshem knew they would find Nehemiah faithfully leading Israel to rebuild the wall around Jerusalem. In the same way, the unbelieving Jewish leaders knew they would find Jesus in the synagogue, teaching; it was "his custom" (Luke 4:16). The predictability of your path of obedience will make you a target for the enemy's snares. That is, of course, if the enemy knows where to find you.

Believers of Christ can be found in church, worshipping the Lord. They can be found singing to the Lord and sharing the message of Jesus Christ. The enemy can always find Christians serving the Lord and speaking the truth in love. They can be found on their knees, crying out to God. They can be found studying the Scriptures early in the morning and obeying them all day long. They can be found "turning the cheek" and serving others in the body of Christ (Matt. 5:39). They can be found humbly confessing their sin.

Will you "take your life into your hands" by living in accordance with God's Word? Will you obey the Lord with such consistency that the enemy knows where to lay the snare? Will you entrust your life to the God who can "save you from the fowler's snare and from the deadly pestilence" (Ps. 91:3)? Do not cower like Saul when God calls you to do something difficult (1 Sam. 10:22). Be careful not to run away like Jonah. God is infinitely worthy of your obedience, no matter the cost. Place your life in His hands today!

My Inheritance

I have inherited your testimonies forever,
for they are the joy of my heart.
I have inclined my heart to do your statutes,
forever to the end.
—Psalm 119:111–112

Father, I don't need a grand inheritance of houses, land, or money. These things don't bring joy to my heart. Still, I confess that my flesh longs for these things. I long for it even though you have already given me everything I need. Guard me from the sin of chasing a larger inheritance. Those who trust in riches "will fall" (Prov. 11:28). Forgive me, Lord, for longing for the things of the world. Your Word is the joy of my heart.

Tonight, I rejoice that you have already blessed me with an inheritance of immeasurable worth. Though "riches do not endure forever …" (Prov. 27:24), your Word will never pass away. You give us everything we need for life and godliness through our knowledge of you (2 Pet. 1:3). Your Word is an inheritance that I could never spend in a million lifetimes. Though I could easily squander an earthly inheritance (Prov. 23:5), your Word will always be enough for me. I will never need to ration this inheritance. The more I enjoy the inheritance of your Word, the more bountiful it becomes to me.

Thankfully, I don't have to die before I share this inheritance with my family. Today I can give it to those I love: a glorious inheritance they will never fight over. Unlike worldly treasures, your Word will sustain and strengthen them for generations. You will bless every part of their lives as they spend their inheritance. Father, "incline my heart" to obey your Word so that I will have a worthy inheritance to leave my family, friends, and neighbors. Help me awake with a renewed desire to revel in the glorious inheritance that you have blessed me with.

Double-Minded

I hate those who are double-minded,
but I love your law.
—Psalm 119:113

God hates duplicity. From the very beginning, God warned Israel, "You shall have no other gods before me" (Exod. 20:3). He admonished Israel, saying, "Fear the LORD your God, serve him only" (Deut. 6:13). Yet Israel disobeyed God and worshipped other gods. Their rebellion prompted the Lord to devastate them by the hands of the Assyrians and Babylonians. And this is not surprising since "a house divided against itself will fall" (Luke 11:17). Sadly, they thought they could mask their sinfulness by maintaining aspects of the law's requirements. But God saw through their hypocrisy, saying, "These people come near to me with their mouth and honor me with their lips, but their hearts are far from me" (Isa. 29:13). God confronted Israel's duplicity through the prophet Elijah, who rebuked them, saying, "How long will you waver between two opinions? If the LORD is God, follow him; but if Baal is God, follow him" (1 Kings 18:21). God will not share His glory with another (Isa. 42:8).

God has called you into an exclusive relationship with Him through the work of Jesus Christ on the cross. By the power of the Holy Spirit, you can live fully committed to Him! Don't underestimate the sinfulness of a divided heart. To the lukewarm church in Laodicea, Jesus said, "I am about to spit you out of my mouth" (Rev. 3:16). The severity of that rebuke is matched in intensity with the warning of

1 John 2:15, "If anyone loves the world, love for the Father is not in him."

Sadly, we have all been duplicitous in our relationship with the Lord. I have personally allowed many things to pollute my pure devotion to Christ. The thoughts of our minds and the affections of our hearts are so easily diverted away from the Lord toward frivolous things in this world. Thankfully, Jesus died to redeem us from the sin of a divided heart.

The antithesis of a "divided" heart can be found in the life of one who loves God's Word. Love for God's Word will cultivate within you "sincere and pure devotion to Christ" (2 Cor. 11:3). Walk in God's truth and He will give you an "undivided heart" that fears His name (Ps. 86:11). It is easy to find those who feign love for the Lord but hard to find those totally devoted to Christ. As Proverbs says, "Many claim to have unfailing love, but a faithful person who can find?" (Prov. 20:6). God's eyes "range throughout the earth to strengthen those who whose hearts are fully committed to him" (2 Chron. 16:9). Will He find you?

My Shield

You are my hiding place and my shield;
I put my hope in your word.
—Psalm 119:114

Father, I confess that I often fail to experience the joy of hiding in you because I do not spend enough time in your Word. It's only as I fix my hope on your Word that I am able to rejoice in you as my refuge and shield. When my time in your Word is lacking, I begin to feel vulnerable and anxious. My mind amplifies problems to outrageous proportions and then works tirelessly to disentangle them, but to no avail. Not realizing the fortress that you are to me, I shrink back from challenges and avoid obstacles. I find myself despairing from even the routine duties that I used to find satisfaction in. Life feels like a dreary exercise in surviving the stress of life when I don't spend time in your Word. But it's not as though I have lost faith in you during times like these. Instead, it feels like my faith is no match for my problems. There is no peace for me when I do not rest in you through your Word. Father, forgive me.

But when I focus my heart and attention on your Word, I find great strength in you as my refuge and shield. Joy and confidence in you replaces the dread over situations outside of my control. Your Word helps me to see how insignificant most of my troubles really are. As I read your Word, you give me a greater understanding of your perfect power. Seeing your power and might in the Scripture changes my perspective to the point that my problems no longer control me. Focusing on you transforms my perspective to the point where I can see you at work in my situation.

Shield me from doubt and anxiety as I plunge into the depths of your Word. As I read and believe your Word, shield me from Satan's deception. Shield me from the "flaming arrows of the evil one" (Eph. 6:16) as your Word galvanizes a stronger faith within me. Shield me from all of the temptation that I have yielded to in the past. Shield me from those in this life that hate you and scoff at my desire to honor you.

As I lie down to rest tonight, I worship you for being my hiding place and my shield. Thank you for guarding and protecting my life and for loving me in all of my weakness. I have put my hope in your precious promises. Tomorrow, help me awake with all of the courage that comes from having rested in you, my refuge.

Go Away

Go away from me evildoers,
that I may keep the commandments of my God.
—Psalm 119:115

You will never achieve an obedient life if you are inappropriately entangled in the sinful lives of the wicked. The struggle to live an obedient life will always require a determination to live with an appropriate measure of separation from evildoers. There was no possibility of the evildoers in Psalm 119 having a positive impact on the psalmist. Whether fearful of their persecution or wary of facing temptation, "Go away from me …" captures his resolve to live his life free from their sinfulness. His desire to walk in obedience to God's Word was not compatible with dwelling among evildoers.

While those called to be "salt and light" cannot live in isolation, they must avoid being unnecessarily entangled with evildoers (Matt. 5:13–14). As Paul warned, "Do not be yoked together with unbelievers. For what do righteousness and wickedness have in common? Or what fellowship can light have with darkness? What harmony is there between Christ and Belial? Or what does a believer have in common with an unbeliever?" (2 Cor. 6:14–15). After all, "bad company corrupts good character" (1 Cor. 15:33).

Far too many Christians compromise their walk with the Lord by dwelling among those who do evil. Those struggling with temptation often hide this folly behind the guise of wanting to influence people for Jesus Christ. But Christians can't impact a dark world for Christ

while being sucked into its filth. Pulling people out of "quicksand"
works so much better when we do not jump into it with them.
Predictably, many weak-willed Christians naively sink into the sinful
mire of those they are attempting to influence, rendering them
ineffective for the cause of Christ.

Never hide from your responsibility to engage a lost world with
the gospel of Jesus Christ. Weep over the lost, pray for them, talk to
them about the Lord, but don't become ensnared by their ways. Forge
relationships with those who need Christ, but never in a manner that
compromises your testimony in the world. The day may come when
you too will have to say, "away from me."

"Blessed is the one who does not walk in step with the wicked
or stand in the way that sinners take or sit in the seat of mockers."

—Psalm 1:1

Sustain

Sustain me according to your word and I will live;
do not let me be ashamed from my hope.
Uphold me and I will be delivered;
I will look on your statutes continually.

—Psalm 119:116–117

Father, thank you for sustaining me by your Word—I cannot sustain myself. Nothing else in life could ever uphold me like your precious promises. If not for your Word, I would have despaired and given up long ago. Frustration, fear, and anxiety are no match for the sustaining power of your Word. I can even trust you to uphold me in the midst of persecution. You will see me through temptation and regret, through guilt and shame, through joy and grief, through sickness and health. You made me, so I know that you will carry me and deliver me (Isa. 46:3–4). For as long as you give me breath, you will support me through every trial in life. You will shepherd me through the "darkest valley" by your promises (Ps. 23). Not even the evil one can overcome the grip that you have on my life—thank you for not letting me go.

By your grace, and because you sustain me, I will not stop trusting and hoping in you. I will not stop believing in Jesus Christ. I will never stop doing the things that you have called me to do. I will not stop loving my brothers and sisters in Christ. I will not stop sharing your Word with others. I will not stop making disciples of all nations. I will never stop going to church. I will not stop tithing. I will not stop praying or reading your Word. I will never stop loving you.

Father, help me to serve you courageously, knowing that you will sustain me. Forgive me for the times that I have recoiled from challenges that required me to trust in your Word. Guard me from ever thinking that I am on my own. Teach me to lean on your sustaining power. Keep me from the sin of trusting in my own abilities. Help me to step out on faith at every juncture. Protect me and those I love as I obey you. Overcome my weaknesses with your perfect power. Tonight, I rest underneath the promise that you will sustain me.

Discarded

You reject all who stray from your statutes,
for their deceitfulness is deception.
You discard all of the wicked of the earth like dross;
therefore, I love your testimonies.
—Psalm 119:118–119

Wickedness is not merely an alternative lifestyle, a disease, or the result of poor self-control. Wickedness is the rejection of God's truth. When a person rejects God's truth, they have made the simultaneous decision to live in deception. Those who exchange "the truth about God for a lie" are "filled with every kind of wickedness, evil, greed and depravity. They are full of envy, murder, strife, deceit and malice. They are gossips, slanderers, God-haters, insolent, arrogant and boastful; they invent ways of doing evil; they disobey their parents; they have no understanding, no fidelity, no love, no mercy" (Rom. 1:25, 29–31). All of the problems in our world stem from the same root cause: the rejection of God's truth.

When we understand wickedness as the Bible does, we begin to see the staggering problem of sin in our world. Our world has rejected God's truth as a worthy standard for living. Naturally, all manner of evil has been the result. As Isaiah said, we "live among a people of unclean lips" (Isa. 6:5). However grim it looks to us, imagine God's perspective. He "looks down from heaven on the sons of men to see if there are any who understand, any who seek God. All have turned aside, they have together become corrupt; there is no one who does good, not even one" (Ps. 14:2–3). As in the days of Sodom, we will see God's judgment poured out in epic proportions on our wicked world.

Those who reject God's Word will be discarded as dross.

In contrast to the wicked, you and I can demonstrate our love for Christ by loving God's Word and rejecting the deceitfulness of this world. Let your love for Jesus Christ drive you relentlessly to His sweet words. Feed on the "words of eternal life" day after day (John 6:68). Meditate on the biblical truths that the world mocks. Sing the very words that make the wicked cringe. Delight in what the lost world abhors. Commit to memory what the world tries so desperately to ignore. Feast on God's Word and He will purify you for the day of redemption.

Trembling

*My flesh trembles from fear of you
and I fear your judgments.*
—Psalm 119:120

Father, I confess that it has been too long since I've trembled at your Word. I delve into your Word for comfort and strength but so often neglect the obedience that you deserve. I would rather fill my mind with encouraging, heartwarming thoughts than change my behavior in radical ways. Ruminating about your plans to bless me seems more enjoyable than repenting so that my life blesses you. I confess that I am quick to make my time in your Word about me. Forgive me for my selfishness.

You "churn up the sea so that its waves roar" (Isa. 51:15). At your presence, the earth trembles and quakes, the foundations of the mountains shake (Ps. 18:7). You expose the "valleys of the sea" and lay bare the "foundations of the earth" with your rebuke (Ps. 18:15). With your power, you split the earth asunder (Isa. 24:19). The world trembles in response to your majestic greatness, yet I so often read your Word and remain motionless. I have read your Word and remained unmotivated to share it with others. I have listened to your truth and refused to worship humbly. I have taken your correction with such nonchalance. When I cannot escape your rebuke, I am mostly troubled at the thought of changing my comfortable routines;

irritation stands in the place of genuine sorrow over sin. Forgive me, Lord.

Grant me grace to respond quickly to your Word. May the slightest whisper of your truth compel me to respond with vigorous obedience. Teach me to live in holy awe of you and your Word. Help me to repent from my listless response to your powerful truth. In the place of my lethargy, fill me with zeal to obey everything you have commanded. May your Holy Spirit awaken me to the joy of obedience and the pain of procrastinating. Help me rise in the morning with a renewed desire to "tremble" at your Word.

Real

I have done justice and righteousness;
do not leave me to my oppressors.
Ensure good for your servant;
do not let the arrogant oppress me.
—Psalm 119:121–122

Is the psalmist bragging when he says, "I have done justice and righteousness"? Certainly not. He does not say this because it makes him deserving of the Lord's help, but because it establishes him as one who belongs to God. Those who belong to God can call out desperately to Him for deliverance. In contrast, God does not promise to answer the prayers of those who have determined that they will cherish sin in their heart (Ps. 66:18). God hides His face from those who "hate good and love evil" (Mic. 3:2–4). Our God is "far from the wicked, but he hears the prayer of the righteous" (Prov. 15:29). Those striving to live righteously can cry out to God for His justice. But those who live in wickedness should not plead for justice to the God who may start with them first.

The most convincing evidence of your faith in Christ is obedience to the Word of God. Your obedience, albeit imperfect, testifies to your faith in the Lord in a way that nothing else can. As 1 John 2:3 teaches, "We know that we have come to know him if we keep his commands." God's love is made complete in those who obey His Word (1 John 2:4). Or put more simply, "this is love for God: to keep his commands" (1 John 5:3). Thankfully, God's grace is larger than our failures.

When you put your faith in Jesus Christ, God longs to hear your prayers, even when you struggle with sin. As you live a life pleasing to the Lord, you can rest in the knowledge that He wants to hear your voice. When we obey Christ, we can "receive from him anything we ask" (1 John 3:22). God beckons His people to prayer, saying, "Call to me and I will answer you and tell you great and unsearchable things you do not know" (Jer. 33:3). And again in 2 Chronicles 7:14: "if my people, who are called by my name, will humble themselves and pray and seek my face and turn from their wicked ways, then will I hear from heaven, and I will forgive their sin and will heal their land."

Since God hears those who belong to Him, cry out to Him daily for strength, for deliverance, and for healing. Pray like the persistent widow who cried out to God for justice unceasingly: "will not God bring about justice for his chosen ones, who cry out to him day and night? Will he keep putting them off?" (Luke 18:7). As God's child, approach His "throne of grace with confidence" so that you "may receive mercy and find grace" (Heb. 4:16).

According to Your Love

My eyes fail for your salvation
and for your righteous word.
Deal with your servant according to your steadfast love
and teach me your statutes.
I am your servant; give me understanding
that I might know your testimonies.
—Psalm 119:123–125

Father, I thank you for dealing with me according to your steadfast love. Though I deserve your wrath, you sent your Son Jesus to die for me. Jesus bore the wrath of God so that those who trust in Him might be saved. By your Holy Spirit, you have enabled me to trust in the work of Christ for the forgiveness of my sin. I rejoice that I am forgiven and loved by you.

Though you have always dealt with me according to your steadfast love, I have not always returned this love to you. I confess my selfishness toward you. I have behaved with immaturity and foolishness. I have not always devoted time to worshipping you. I confess that I have squandered my time with vain entertainment. I have failed to believe you and trust in your Word. I have been slothful in my prayer life. Your love is steadfast, but mine is fickle at times.

Deal with your servant according to your steadfast love in every area of my life. Deal with me according to your love in death and in sorrow. Extend your love to me when I feel overwhelmed and anxious. Deal with me according to your love when I feel threatened. Give me your love when I am angry. Display your steadfast love to me when I feel exhausted or defeated. Show your love to me when I sense the shame of my sin. Deal with me according to your love when I am lonely and afraid.

Show your love to me by teaching me your Word. Give your servant understanding in the Scriptures. I will never understand the scope of your love for me without understanding your Word. I will never be able to love you as you deserve without understanding your Word. I cannot separate your love for me or my love for you from your Word. Tonight, I rest underneath your powerful love.

It Is Time

It is time for you to act, Oh Lord,
they have broken your law.
—Psalm 119:126

Those who persistently break God's law will eventually provoke Him toward action. God is "compassionate and gracious … slow to anger, abounding in love and faithfulness, maintaining love to thousands, and forgiving wickedness, rebellion and sin. Yet he does not leave the guilty unpunished …" (Exod. 34:6–7). For centuries, Christians have leaned on the righteousness of God when facing the appalling forces of evil. God does not expect you to fix the problem of evil in our world. Instead, He calls you to pray. For centuries, those who have suffered underneath cruel oppression have prayed, "O Lord God Almighty, the God of Israel, rouse yourself to punish all the nations …" (Ps. 59:5). This prayerful chorus will continue into the tribulation, when those who've been slain because of their testimony cry out, "How long, Sovereign Lord, holy and true, until you judge the inhabitants of the earth and avenge our blood?" (Rev. 6:9–10). God has heard and continues to hear these prayers.

We live in an age of unfettered wickedness. The torrents of immorality grow stronger with every generation. Vulnerable children around the world face the jaws of sex trafficking. The sin of homosexuality has been normalized and even celebrated as an acceptable lifestyle. Violent crime, drugs, and sexual immorality threaten every community. Despite unprecedented technological advances, starvation and preventable diseases rage around the world. In many places corruption and greed hinder humanitarian aid in communities stricken with poverty. Islamic terrorists have beheaded, crucified, and burned Christians alive in the name of a false god. Yet the womb continues to be one of the most hostile environments, in that millions of babies are murdered every year.

While living in this sinful world, pray for the gospel to advance among those who will believe and turn from their sins. Share the good news of salvation through Jesus Christ with whoever will listen. But for those who refuse to turn to Jesus for salvation, join the chorus of those who for centuries have prayed, "your kingdom come, your will be done" (Matt. 6:10); "repay them for what their hands have done and bring back on them what they deserve" (Ps. 28:4); "Rise up, Judge of the earth; pay back to the proud what they deserve" (Ps. 94:2); "Come, Lord Jesus" (Rev. 22:20); "reign in righteousness" (Isa. 32:1); "may all your enemies perish, LORD" (Judg. 5:31); "May God arise, may his enemies be scattered …" (Ps. 68:1); and, "It is time for you to act, Oh Lord, they have broken your law" (Ps. 119:126).

Upright

Therefore, I love your commandments more than gold,
more than fine gold.
Therefore, all of your precepts are upright;
I hate every false path.
—Psalm 119:127–128

Father, I love your commandments more than gold because they are upright. The riches of this world have no intrinsic worth (Eccles. 2:8–11). In a world filled with deception and moral bankruptcy, your Word is eternally upright. Your Word is the only standard for what is truly upright. It is only in studying your Word that I am able to see all that is crooked in the world.

Nevertheless, I confess that I have longed for and even loved things that are false and worthless. Forgive me for attributing worth to things that have none. Thank you for slaying your Son to redeem me from my love of sin. Through your Word and the ministry of the Holy Spirit, teach me to hate "pride and arrogance, evil behavior and perverse speech" (Prov. 8:13).

Help me to demonstrate my love for your Word by meditating on it. Discipline my mind to consider "whatever is true, whatever is noble, whatever is right, whatever is pure, whatever is lovely, whatever is admirable" as well as all things "excellent or praiseworthy" (Phil. 4:8). While nothing in this world meets these criteria, your Word epitomizes them. Give me grace to understand just how "upright" your Word truly is so that I can see through the "crooked" things of this world. Remind me to test the value of every activity in life against the plumb line of your truth. Give me resolve to discard things that do not measure up to your standard.

Grant me the opportunity to encourage fellow believers to love your Word more than the things of this world. In a spirit of humility and grace, use me to open people's eyes to the truth of your Word. Help me to live the kind of life that celebrates all that is true in your Word and repudiates all that is false in this world.

The Simple

Your testimonies are wonderful;
therefore, my soul keeps them.
The unfolding of your word gives light,
giving understanding to the simple.

—Psalm 119:129–130

Those who ignore God's Word are destined to remain "simple." Though we commonly consider simplicity a positive attribute, the biblical understanding of the term is much different. The word "simple" in the Bible does not mean aesthetically minimalistic, uncomplicated, or modest. Instead, the term repeatedly refers to those who are "ignorant and foolish" (Prov. 1:22, 8:5, 14:18). Simplicity is not quite as harmless as it might sound. The simple fall prey to the adulteress (Prov. 7:7). The simple believe anything (Prov. 14:15) and inherit folly (Prov. 14:18). The simple do not have the sense to avoid danger (Prov. 22:3). Instead, they live sinfully and eventually die because of it (Prov. 1:32).

The ignorance of the simple cannot be solved by academic achievements. Sophistication and intellect only mask the severity of spiritual ignorance. Not even one's vast experience can remedy foolishness. Long life merely gives one's folly time to compound. Not even religious activity can overcome the deficiencies of the simple. God's Word is the only solution for the simple. What a shame to live in hopeless ignorance when God's Word offers a wealth of wisdom. Wisdom beckons the simple to drink from the well of understanding: "Leave your simple ways and you will live; walk in the way of insight" (Prov. 9:6).

There is wonderful light and understanding available for you in God's Word. Though God's thoughts are infinitely higher (Isa. 55:9), you can have the "mind of Christ" (1 Cor. 2:16). If you have been delivered from "darkened ... understanding," persevere in the light of God's Word (Eph. 4:18). "[B]e wise about what is good, and innocent about what is evil" (Rom. 16:19). "[W]alk in the light, as he is in the light ..." (1 John 1:7). Read God's Word and draw near to Jesus, the light of the world (John 8:12).

Panting

I open wide my mouth and pant,
for I long for your commandments.
—Psalm 119:131

Father, I was taught to read your Word and memorize your Word, but not to pant after it. Looking around, there have never been many examples of people living in desperation for your Word. So often I fall into the trap of reading just enough of your Word so that I can get by. I need much more than a passion for your Word; I need to realize my desperation for you. My passion might ebb and flow, but desperation will create an abiding commitment.

I need you as I need food and water. I cannot live the Christian life without your Word. I cannot live a life that glorifies you without your Word. I cannot even have a close relationship with you without your Word. I cannot lead a fully repentant life without your Word. I cannot experience victory over sin while ignoring your Word. I cannot live wisely without the counsel of your Word. I cannot accomplish all that you have planned for me (Eph. 2:10) without your Word. I cannot worship you the way you deserve without feasting on your Word. I cannot even pray as you want me to pray if I don't read the Bible. I cannot enjoy the abundant life without your Word.

Yet the knowledge of my desperation fades as I turn to other things in this life. Gradually, my heart begins to pant after things that do not meet my needs. I have panted after achievement and success. I have panted after money and possessions. I have panted after people's approval and acceptance. I have panted after relaxation and entertainment. Thank you for convicting me of my sin and giving me grace to turn from it. Though I am not free from these temptations, I yearn for more of you. Teach me to thirst for you "As the deer pants for streams of water" (Ps. 42:1). Help me to open wide my mouth for your Word (Ps. 81:10).

Established

Turn to me and be gracious,
as is fitting for those who love your name.

Establish my footsteps in your word,
and do not let any iniquity rule over me.

Redeem me from the oppression of men
that I may keep your precepts.

—Psalm 119:132–134

In the absence of a relationship with Jesus Christ and the empowering presence of the Holy Spirit in a person's life, sin rules. It's not that unbelievers sin too much, it's that they are enslaved to it (Rom. 7:14). The Scripture says, "wickedness will not release those who practice it" (Eccles. 8:8). Jesus himself said, "everyone who sins is a slave to sin" (John 8:34). But Christ came to set us free from this hopeless bondage!

Those who come to God through faith in Jesus Christ are liberated from their slavery to sin. "It is for freedom that Christ has set us free …" (Gal. 5:1). Paul even goes so far as to say we are dead to sin when we are baptized into Jesus Christ (Rom. 6:2). Our freedom affords us the privilege of a new glorious slavery to Jesus Christ (Rom. 7:25). If we are liberated from the power of sin in our lives, why do we still struggle with sinful behavior?

Without question, believers still struggle with sin. In fact, "If we claim to be without sin, we deceive ourselves and the truth is not in us" (1 John 1:8). Genuine believers in Christ have given themselves to drunkenness, drug addiction, and all manner of sexual sin. Christians have become entangled in rage, malice, envy, deception, and slander to the point where it is difficult to see any modicum of faith in Christ. Paul himself found himself doing the sinful things that he hated: "For what I do is not the good I want to do, but the evil I do not want to do—this I keep on doing" (Rom. 7:19). Paul's story is my story—and yours as well. Knowing the difficulty of our struggle with sin, we would be foolish to fight it without God's Word.

A life of victory over sin cannot be separated from seeking God through His Word. God wants to establish your footsteps in His Word. This is one of the ways that God shows His grace to you. God calls you to be firmly committed and disciplined in His Word, yet ultimately it is God's grace that establishes your footsteps. Sin will not rule you as you trust in Christ and walk with Him through His Word. As you consistently spend time in God's Word, you can pray with eager expectation, "do not let … iniquity rule over me." But if you battle sin without a commitment to God's Word, you will surely fail. May God establish you in His Word today!

Learning to Weep

*Cause your face to shine on your servant
and teach me your statutes.
Streams of tears pour from my eyes
because they have not kept your law.*
—Psalm 119:135–136

Father, when you teach me your Word, it is as though the radiance of your face is shining on me. When you illuminate your Word to my mind, I see the face of Christ more clearly. Your love, mercy, justice, kindness, and power become clearer to me when you reveal your Word to me. You taught Aaron and his descendants to pray that you would cause your face to shine upon Israel—this divine blessing had everything to do with you teaching them to obey your Word. How can any of us even recognize your beauty if we don't see you in Scripture? As I revel in the wonder of your Word, I cannot help but grieve when I consider the world around me. Your Word helps me see you for who you are and the world for what it is.

I weep over the horrific slaughter of the unborn in their mother's womb. I hurt for the millions of children who are born into debilitating poverty because of the violence, corruption, and greed of those in power. I grieve over the violent abuse that children suffer around the world. I am overwhelmed with sorrow as I think of the brutality toward Christians around the world. I weep because people "have not kept your law."

I also weep because of the sinfulness within the people of God. My heart is heavy over the indifference that your people demonstrate toward your Word. I have grave concern for those who are so interested in their hobbies that they do not serve you with any measure of faithfulness. I weep because Christians slander one another. I grieve when Christians leave churches over petty differences. I weep when Christians hold on to bitterness and refuse to forgive others. I am grieved over my own sins as well.

As you shine your face on me, give me understanding in your Word. Teach me to weep. Help me to "grieve, mourn and wail. Change [my] laughter to mourning" (James 4:9). I claim the promise, "Blessed are those who mourn, for they will be comforted" (Matt. 5:4).

Tested

You are righteous, Oh Lord,
and your judgments are upright.

You have commanded your testimonies in righteousness
and in exceeding faithfulness.

My zeal consumes me,
for my enemies have forgotten your words.

Your word has been tested exceedingly and your servant loves it.

—Psalm 119:137–140

Every generation must answer the question for themselves: "Is God's Word true?" The question elicits slanderous criticisms of God's Word among enemies of the cross. Cultural elites take pleasure in ridiculing the "crude" and "unenlightened" book. Credentialed scholars and philosophers mock the so-called "unsophisticated" teachings of the Scripture. Elected officials who identify themselves as Christians work strategically to avoid the appearance of affirming verses that are no longer politically correct. Their moderated positions become the norm in a society that refuses to accept the whole counsel of God. Many who were raised in church will run quickly from their spiritual roots toward more pluralistic philosophies of God that do not elicit social consequences. Pastors of every denomination unfortunately lead the apostasy by teaching only what "itching ears want to hear" (2 Tim. 4:3).

The centuries-long, satanic assault on the Word of God has only succeeded in revealing its inestimable worth. Hundreds of thousands of churches feast every week on the divine diet of God's Word. As a result, God is raising up an army of believers to advance the gospel of Jesus Christ around the world. God's Word emboldens believers to be faithful in sharing the good news and to give their lives for Christ. Despite the perpetual assault on the Bible, God continues to transform lives as people read His Word. Those entangled in the mire of sin find freedom, forgiveness, grace, and mercy. God's Word still gives hope, strength, and peace in the midst of our tumultuous world. God's Word is still fueling the most joyous worship of our risen Savior around the world. God's Word has been exceedingly tested and it has been proved righteous and upright. May zeal for God and His Word consume you today.

Despised

I am small and despised;
I have not forgotten your precepts.
Your righteousness is an eternal righteousness
and your law is true.
Distress and anguish have found me;
your commandments are my delight.
Your testimonies are righteous for eternity;
give me understanding that I may live.
—Psalm 119:141–144

Father, I choose to be lowly and despised for the sake of Jesus Christ. Out of love for you, I will endure distress and anguish. In the midst of the enemy's attack, I will not forget your Word. In fact, your Word will sustain me in the midst of my distress. I will not allow pain in my life to eclipse the joy of knowing you through your Word. Your Word can overwhelm the misery of any situation. I rejoice that my hardships cannot rob me of the abundant life you make available to me through the work of Jesus Christ (John 10:10). In the midst of injustice, I can delight in your eternal righteousness. Give me understanding in your Word so that I can experience the life that you have made possible for me in Christ.

Forgive me for the ways in which I have disobeyed you in order to avoid the hostility of those around me. I also confess that I have not always responded well to opposition. Instead of delighting in your Word and rising above my circumstances, I have felt sorry for myself. I have whined and complained. Other times I have lashed out in anger instead of forgiving and praying for those who wronged me. I rejoice in the righteousness of Jesus Christ that you have given me.

I am weak, but you are powerful to make things right in the world. As wars rage around the world, I trust in your eternal righteousness. As corruption causes the most vulnerable to suffer, I trust in your eternal righteousness. As wicked men rise to power, I trust in your eternal righteousness. As Christians suffer for their faith around the world, I trust in your eternal righteousness. As violent crime rages around me, I trust in your eternal righteousness. Tonight, I rest in your perfect righteousness.

Crying Out

I call with all of my heart: answer me,
Oh Lord, and I will keep your statutes.

I call out to you, save me
and I will keep your testimonies.

I rise early in the morning and I cry for help;
I have put my hope in your word.

—Psalm 119:145–147

Where have the desperate cries of the church gone? Prayer has become a perfunctory, religious ritual used primarily to start and end church activities. Sadly, there are precious few who are comfortable attending meetings where the only aim is prayer. And when meetings are held specifically for the purpose of prayer, they so often deviate from their purpose into forums for prayer requests and updates about church members. Even pastors would much rather preach a sermon than fall on their knees and cry out to God in a spirit of humble desperation. Jesus said, "My house will be called a house of prayer for all nations," (Mark 11:17) yet the thought of devoting ourselves in any serious way to prayer seems unsophisticated and uncomfortable. Sadly, many would rather complain about those who want to remove prayer from schools than address the prayerlessness in churches. In this climate, we would do well to learn from the psalmist's prayer life.

The psalmist cried out with all of his heart not because he doubted God would hear him, but because he knew God would answer. If we believe God hears and answers, then we will fill our church and the ears of our Master with zealous prayer. But we will never sustain a zealous prayer life with an anemic commitment to God's Word.

Intermingled with the description of his prayer life, the psalmist says, "I will keep your statutes … I will keep your testimonies … I have put my hope in your Word."

Do you cry out with all of your heart? Do you rise at midnight to cry for help? Do you relentlessly cast yourself at the Lord's feet as a desperate pauper? Or has your prayer life degenerated into a well-mannered religious exercise that you only employ at convenient times and places? Spend your day crying out to God!

Night Watches

My eyes anticipate the night watches,
to meditate on your word.
—Psalm 119:148

Father, I confess that I am so often exhausted by the demands of life. I sometimes give in to the frenetic pace of life and fail to spend the focused time that I need in your Word. While I am thankful for every blessing that keeps me busy during the day, I end most days completely fatigued. Thank you for the rest that you give me each night (Eccles. 5:12). I know that you made me to need rest and that you grant sleep to those you love (Ps. 127:2). There are times, though, when I need to spend the night watches with you, the God who never sleeps (Ps. 121:3–4). As you called the disciples to keep watch in the Garden of Gethsemane (Matt. 26:38), help me not to miss out on opportunities to meditate on your words.

Guard me from loving sleep in an unhealthy way (Prov. 6:9). Those who love sleep grow poor (Prov. 20:13, 24:33). Help me to never use sleep as an excuse to delay acts of obedience (Ps. 132:3–4; Prov. 6:4). Give me strength to deny my flesh during times when my famished spirit needs more attention than my weary body.

May the sweetness of your presence draw me occasionally in the watches of the night. If I awaken in the middle of the night, keep me from squandering the time with anxious thoughts. Instead, help me dwell on your Word until you return me to sleep. Calm me with your promises in the still of the night. Awaken me to remind me of your Word. Arouse me from my sleep to teach me Scripture. Keep me from sleeping through powerful encounters with you. May the joy of spending time in your Word strengthen me beyond what my sleep would've afforded me. In those quiet moments in the night, help me experience the fullness of resting in Christ.

Far

Hear my voice according to your steadfast love,
Oh Lord, give me life according to your judgments.
Those who pursue evil draw near;
they are far from your law.

—Psalm 119:149–150

The proliferation of evil in our world means that the wicked have never been closer to you than they are today. You are surrounded by people who use God's name as a curse. The streets of your neighborhood are filled with those who do not fear God. The roads of your city are crowded with those who lie and steal. Your culture is saturated with unbridled covetousness and idolatry. Whatever paltry amount of spirituality exists in your community is likely reserved for the worship of false gods. Everywhere you turn, people are filling themselves with the lustrous vanity of our world. But their wickedness is far from harmless. Sexual deviants and violent criminals pounce on the defenseless among us. Not only are these people evil, but they actively pursue evil. In fact, they "invent ways of doing evil" (Rom. 1:30).

Many philosophize and postulate as to what causes a person to plunge willingly into the bog of such depravity. Should we blame their parents for failing to discipline or perhaps the noxious influence of their friends? Maybe the educational system failed them. Perhaps the wicked were drawn to violence by the movies they watch or the music they listen to. Maybe the immoral were bereft of care and compassion as children. Though these may all be reasonable lines of inquiry, the single most important reason for wicked behavior lies in Psalm 119:150.

Though the wicked are inseparable from their evil deeds, they are far from God's Word. The Word of God is never on their hearts, never on their minds, and never on their tongues. They don't read God's Word, memorize God's Word, or study God's Word. In rejecting the Bible they have rejected the God of the Bible. Tragically, many who identify themselves as "Christians" are not far from this same description. It is impossible to be far from Scripture and close to God. Don't allow a distance between you and God's Word. Draw near to God through His Word today!

Near

You are near, Oh Lord,
and all of our commandments are true.
Long ago I have known from your testimonies
that you established them for eternity.
—Psalm 119:151–152

Father, no matter how close the enemy comes, I take comfort in the promise that you are near. You are always near to those who call on you in truth (Ps. 145:18). I rejoice that you sent your Holy Spirit to live with me forever (John 14:16–17). Thank you for never leaving or forsaking me (Josh. 1:5). "Where can I go from your Spirit? Where can I flee from your presence? If I go up to the heavens, you are there; if I make my bed in the depths, you are there. If I rise on the wings of the dawn, if I settle on the far side of the sea, even there your hand will guide me, your right hand will hold me fast. If I say, 'Surely the darkness will hide me and the light become night around me,' even the darkness will not be dark to you; the night will shine like the day, for darkness is as light to you" (Ps. 139:7–12).

Though I know that you are always with me, sometimes I feel alone. Few if any understand the things that trouble me. So often those who might empathize are fully engaged in their own trials. Oddly, I don't always seek you when I feel lonely. I confess that I try to mask my discontentment with trivial diversions that only exacerbate my situation. Disciplined time in your Word sometimes wanes during these difficult seasons.

When "there is no one to help" and "trouble is near," "do not be far from me" (Ps. 22:11). Awaken me to the reality of your presence tomorrow morning as I read your Word. May the renewed awareness of your presence encourage me toward obedience and worship. Overwhelm whatever fear the enemy tries to confront me with. By the power of your Holy Spirit, help me to be a courageous witness for Jesus Christ tomorrow (Acts 1:8).

Plead My Cause

Look upon my affliction and deliver me,
for I have not forgotten your law.

Plead my cause and redeem me;
give me life according to your word.

—Psalm 119:153–154

When you stand for what is true and Holy, God will contend for your cause. The Creator of the Universe will intervene to accomplish what is right and just. The Judge of the Earth, in His perfect timing, will rise up and "pay back to the proud what they deserve" (Ps. 94:2). The Lord will plead your case against those who malign what is just.

God's involvement, however, does not guarantee that you will evade the personal suffering that accompanies standing for truth. In fact, refusing to deny God's righteous standard in this world may cost you your life. But not even your death means victory for the wicked. God will have the final word. When Christ returns to the earth, He will reign in righteousness (Isa. 32:1). God will execute His justice for the rest of eternity.

Most of your quarrels in life, however, probably have little to do with righteous causes. If you are like most people, you find yourself quibbling over inconsequential offenses that amount to nothing. Don't expect the Ruler of the Universe to defend the selfish cause of one who refuses to forgive and extend mercy. Ask yourself, "Is my dispute a defense of God's standard or my preferences?" If it is a righteous cause, consider whether or not you have represented it in a righteous manner. God wants you to "get rid of all bitterness, rage and anger, brawling and slander, along with every form of malice" (Eph. 4:31).

Before you start your day, ask God to help you forgive those who have offended you. Pray also that God will enable them to forgive you. Don't lob friendly fire on your brothers and sisters in Christ. Stand united as you face the wickedness of the world. Join with your fellow believers and "contend for the faith" with unbending resolve (Jude 1:3). In every situation where you find yourself standing up for what is right, trust that God will contend for your cause.

Day 35 — Evening

Far from the Wicked

Salvation is far from the wicked,
for they do not seek your statutes.
—Psalm 119:155

Father, tonight I pray for those in my life who are still so far from salvation. They are far from salvation because they reject your Word. They reject the hope of Jesus Christ. They reject the reality of their sin. They refuse to contemplate in any serious way what your Word has to say about hell. They mock the notion that their sin deserves eternal separation from you. They dismiss your miraculous power described in the Bible as irrational and illogical. They refuse to accept that you loved them enough to send your Son Jesus to die on the cross. Filled with false hopes of personal goodness, they will spend eternity in hell unless you intervene and draw them closer to the truth of your Word.

I confess that I do not have the ability to nudge their hearts closer to you. I cannot make them acknowledge their sin and repent. Though I ask you to help me to be faithful to tell them about the gospel of Jesus Christ, I know that I cannot convince them to place their trust in Jesus for the forgiveness of their sin. Thankfully, "With man this is impossible, but with God all things are possible" (Matt. 19:26).

Father, I pray that you would remove their heart of stone and give them a new heart, filled with your Spirit (Ezek. 36:26). Convict them of sin and their need for repentance. Give them eyes to see your great grace and love. Help them to hate their sin. Incite them to call out to you for forgiveness and mercy. "Everyone who calls on the name of the Lord will be saved" (Rom. 10:13). Draw them close to you each day through your Word and prayer. By the power of your Holy Spirit, bring those who are far from you close; make them your children.

I rejoice tonight that you have brought me into a relationship with you. Thank you for revealing yourself to me through your Word. You have given me faith in Jesus Christ for the forgiveness of my sin. Though salvation is far from the wicked, it is near to me.

Many Compassions

Your compassions are many, Oh Lord,
give me life according to your judgments.

My persecutors and my distress are many;
I have not turned from your testimonies.

—Psalm 119:156–157

What in all of creation could comfort a man facing death at the hands of his enemy? Personal armor, defense forces, fortifications, or perhaps a battle plan? No, the psalmist clings to God's love. Although those who oppose Christians are "many," God's compassions are also "many." God's love is more powerful than the enemy's venomous hatred toward Christians.

It's not only that God loves, but that His love for you is great! He is "full of compassion" (Ps. 116:5) and "abounding in love" (Exod. 34:6) for you. The Scripture even teaches that He "crowns you with love and compassion" (Ps. 103:4). His love for you is "higher than the heavens" (Ps. 108:4). God loved you so much "that he gave his one and only Son" for you (John 3:16). He crushed His own Son on the cross so that you might believe in Him and be saved (Isa. 53). God lavished His love on you in Christ so that you might become His child (1 John 3:1). His love for you is incomprehensible. Just as astronomers cannot measure the expanse of space or the number of stars, you cannot comprehend the scope of God's love for you on your own. You need God's divine power to comprehend it. Paul prayed for the Ephesians to have "power … to grasp how wide and long and high and deep is the love of Christ" (Eph. 3:18).

God's love for you is bigger than your challenges and deeper than your problems. It is infinitely larger than your fear and anxiety. God's love is more powerful than your circumstances and more important than people's approval. God's love for you is bigger than your wounds and weaknesses. It is mightier than your failures.

Love Christ back! Demonstrate your love for the Lord by not turning from His Word. In the face of opposition, remain steadfast in your commitment to Scripture. Determine not to let the world deter you from lavishing love on the Lord. Worship Him, follow Him, serve Him today!

All

I look on the faithless and I loathe them
because they do not keep your word.
See that I love your precepts, Oh Lord,
give me life according to your steadfast love.
All of your words are true
and all of your righteous judgments are eternal.
—Psalm 119:158–160

Father, my heart would be riddled with fear and doubt if any portion of your Word was not fully true. I would fear for my salvation if I could not trust your Word. I would stop reading and believing your Word if only some of it was true. I would never take time to memorize and meditate on the Scriptures if there was any mixture of error in it. If your Word was not completely true, I would never share it with others. If there was any possibility of lies in the Bible, it would be like so many other irrelevant religious books. I would give it a cursory reading then set it on my bookshelf and ignore it. But your Word is thoroughly true.

I bless your name for speaking nothing but the truth to me through your Word. Thank you that your Word is totally true from cover to cover. All sixty-six books of the Bible are filled with nothing but truth. Because all of your words are true, I choose to love them, read them, and obey them. I will hang my eternity on the precious promises of your Word. The truthfulness of your Word gives me strength to live life.

Because all of your words are true, I will not live my life in fear and doubt. I will not doubt that I will spend eternity with you. I will not doubt your forgiveness, your mercy, or your grace. I will not doubt that you love and care for me. I will not doubt your power to save. I will not doubt what Jesus did for me on the cross. I will not doubt the power of the resurrection. I will not doubt your presence in my life. The truthfulness of your Word helps me live above the misery of doubt.

Deception

Rulers persecute me without cause,
but my heart trembles at your word.
I rejoice over your words as one who finds great riches.
I hate and abhor deception but I love your law.

—Psalm 119:161–163

It's easy to wink at the seemingly "harmless" sin of deception. Unlike many sins, there is not always an immediate consequence for those who lie. In fact, many lies are never even detected by others. In some situations, it may temporarily appear that lying helps smooth things over. Added with the personal "benefits" of getting oneself out of difficult situations, many have sunk into patterns of deception in their daily lives. Few lose any sleep over representing themselves in contradictory ways to different groups of people. Giving partial truths is deemed equally innocuous in the eyes of many. People feel justified when they lie to "protect" their children from the consequences of their actions. Complaints about government corruption and the mismanagement of revenue is enough for some to rationalize falsifying their annual tax returns. I have known people that lie with such frequency that it seems like second nature to them. One thing is clear: deception is not harmless. Let's see what the Bible teaches about lies.

Those who deceive others will not prosper. Deception among God's people profanes God's name (Lev. 19:11–12). Through deception, false prophets led Israel to think that they could continue in sin without any consequence (Jer. 29:8). But those who lie will eat the fruit of their deception (Hosea 10:13). The wrath of God is coming on those who deceive (Eph. 5:6). Those who live in perpetual deception bear the likeness of Satan himself, who is the "father of lies" (John 8:44). Revelation 21:27 teaches that no one "who does what is shameful or deceitful" will inherit heaven.

Thankfully, Jesus died to save liars. Having been cleansed of this unrighteousness, learn to "hate and abhor deception." Confess the sin of manipulating the truth to suit your agenda. Learn to hate what is false about this world and to love the truth of God's Word. Be truthful even when it hurts. Cling to the truth of God's Word, and "the truth will set you free" (John 8:32).

Great Peace

*Seven times in the day I praise you
for your righteous judgments.
Great peace have those who love your law
and nothing makes them stumble.*
—Psalm 119:164–165

Thank you, Father, for giving me "great peace." I rejoice tonight that I have peace with you through the work of your Son, Jesus Christ (Rom. 5:1; Col. 1:20). Though the "mind governed by the flesh is death" … "the mind controlled by the Spirit is life and peace" (Rom. 8:6). Nothing else in this world compares with the peace that you give. Your peace "transcends all understanding" and guards my heart and mind (Phil. 4:7). All the money in the world cannot buy the peace that I have through Christ. Thank you that I will have the opportunity to experience this peace for the rest of eternity.

Spending time with you through your Word helps me experience the peace that you have given me through Christ. When I neglect your Word, I do not feel peaceful. I struggle with fear and frustration when I am not reading your Word. Even things that should not bother me cause anxiety when I don't read your Word. And when I do read your Word but refuse to obey it, I find the same problem. Help me to love your Word and walk in the peace that you have afforded me through the shed blood of Jesus Christ! Keep me from stumbling as I read your Word.

I know that you have not given me this peace just for my personal benefit. I am surrounded by those who live with enmity toward you. Sadly, many of them will die and spend the rest of eternity separated from you in hell. I remember tonight that you have given me "the ministry of reconciliation" (2 Cor. 5:18). Help me to be your ambassador in the world by telling people that they can have peace with God through Jesus. Guard me from the sin of withholding the precious gospel from those who need to hear it. Tomorrow, help me to awake eager to witness to others.

Waiting

I wait for your salvation, Oh Lord,
and I do your commandments.

My soul keeps your testimonies
and I love them exceedingly.

—Psalm 119:166–167

Some of the most tumultuous times in your life can be characterized by waiting. If you are like most people, you have a difficult time waiting. Not only are we naturally impatient, but fear and doubt can overwhelm us as time passes. It's so easy to grumble and despair during seasons of waiting, yet seasons of waiting are inevitable. Having poured your heart out to the Lord, you will wait for God to answer prayers in His perfect timing (Ps. 5:3). You will wait for the Lord to give you direction in life. You will also have to wait along with every other believer for Christ to return to this world. Until Christ returns, you will wait for Him to judge the wicked and save the righteous. But how can you wait for the Lord in a manner that honors Him?

Surrounded by his enemies, the psalmist determined that he would wait for the Lord's salvation by obeying God's commandments. Waiting is not about being sedentary and passive in your spiritual life, but about actively obeying God's Word (Ps. 37:34). Resist the temptation to become lethargic and frustrated as you wait. You may be in a hurry, but God is not. He wants to make you more like His Son Jesus during seasons of waiting. Determine to learn everything He wants you to learn as you wait.

Are you waiting for something in your life? Seasons of waiting are great opportunities to pore over Scripture. As you wait, learn "to say

'No' to ungodliness and worldly passions, and to live self-controlled, upright and godly lives" (Titus 2:12–13). As you wait, use your spiritual gifts to serve the Lord (1 Cor. 1:7). Wait like the farmer who works diligently in preparation for the rain and crops (James 5:7). Wait for the Lord by trusting and rejoicing in Him (Ps. 33:20). Wait for the Lord by walking in the way of God's laws (Isa. 26:8). May your season of waiting be filled with God's Word.

Known to You

I keep your precepts and your testimonies,
for all of my ways are before you.
—Psalm 119:168

Father, most people around me rebel in plain sight, not thinking that you notice. They push the boundaries of sin in their life, thinking that you are blind. They use their mouths for evil, thinking you cannot hear. But you see, hear, and know everything. You teach me in your Word, "Nothing in all creation is hidden from God's sight. Everything is uncovered and laid bare before the eyes of him to whom we must give an account" (Heb. 4:13). Not one thing has ever escaped your notice: "The eyes of the LORD are everywhere, keeping watch on the wicked and the good" (Prov. 15:3). This is a frightening and disturbing thought for those who reject you, but I take comfort in your watchful eyes.

I know that you see me when I sin, but I take great comfort in the fact that Jesus took the pain and the punishment that my sin deserves. Because you saved me by sending Jesus to the cross, I don't have to hide from you like Adam and Eve in the garden (Gen. 3:8). Instead I can say, "Look to me, Lord, with your loving eyes and lead me by your Spirit to a holy life." But you don't just see my failures. You also see the ways that I am striving to please you. So, tonight, "Look at me, Father, and see how I have kept your precepts."

Watch how my heart has believed in your Word. Take notice of how I read your Word and meditate on it. Listen to me sing your truth with my brothers and sisters in Christ. Hear me slowly memorizing the Scriptures. Pay attention as I desperately claim your promises. Incline your ear to me as I pray the words of the Bible back to you. Watch me share your truth with others. Watch me fast and pray desperately for you to move in my church. As I lie down for the night, "Search me, God, and know my heart; test me and know my anxious thoughts. See if there is any offensive way in me, and lead me in the way everlasting" (Ps. 139:23–24).

Lips

May my cry reach you, Oh Lord,
give me understanding according to your word.

May my supplication come before you;
deliver me according to your word.

My lips will pour out praise,
for you have taught me your statutes.

My tongue will sing of your word,
for all of your commandments are righteous.

—Psalm 119:169–172

What will you do with your mouth today? Are you going to complain about things or pray about them? Will you gossip about others or affirm them? Are you going to criticize your brothers and sisters in Christ or thank God for them? Will you use your tongue to support or undermine spiritual authority? Are you going to fill your conversations with negative sarcasm or encouragement? Will you use your tongue for lies or truth? How will you talk about your family members and coworkers? Will your mouth speak of forgiveness or revenge toward those who have hurt you? You have a choice as to how you will use your mouth today.

Difficult times sometimes bring the worst out of our mouths. We tend to let our tongues run wild when we are troubled or angry. I know that I have said things that I deeply regret. Sadly, we can do a lot of damage when we respond this way. James cautions us from having an unbridled tongue in saying, "Consider what a great forest is set on fire by a small spark. The tongue … is a fire, a world of evil among the parts of the body. It corrupts the whole body, sets the whole course of one's life on fire, and is itself set on fire by hell" (James 3:5–6). When facing difficult times, we need to remember how the psalmist disciplined his mouth.

He determined to sing, pray, and worship the Lord. Knowing that God hears every prayer, spend this day crying out to the Lord. Ask the Lord for understanding as you open His Word. Take your frustration to the Lord and ask Him for help. Instead of grumbling about your circumstances, ask the Lord to move mountains and believe Him to do it. Let your lips overflow with praise to your heavenly Father. Praise Him for being faithful to teach you His Word. Praise Him for powerfully revealing to you His perfect truth. Let your mouth be so full of praise that you don't have time to be critical of others. May this constant spirit of praise overwhelm every worry and fear. Use your tongue to sing about God's righteous Word. Sing about God's promises, God's goodness, and God's power. Today, "keep your tongue from evil and your lips from telling lies" (Ps. 34:13). Use your mouth to encourage those around you (Heb. 3:13). May your "conversation be always full of grace, seasoned with salt" (Col. 4:6). Let the world see Christ in your words today!

Your Hand

May your hand help me,
for I have chosen your precepts.
—Psalm 119:173

Father, you have accomplished "great and awesome deeds" with your "mighty hand and an outstretched arm" (Deut. 4:34). You formed Adam from the dust and created everything by your mighty hand (Gen. 2:7; Acts 7:50). You redeemed Israel out of bondage and destroyed the Egyptians with your mighty hand. "You open your hand and satisfy the desires of every living thing" (Ps. 145:16). I confess that "your right hand [is] exalted" (Ps. 89:13). You guide your children and hold them fast (Ps. 139:10), so that "no one can snatch them" away (John 10:29). Lord Jesus, you touched and healed lepers (Luke 5:13). You gave sight to the blind (Matt. 20:34). You enabled the mute to speak (Mark 7:32). You touched the coffin of a dead boy and brought him back to life (Luke 7:12).

Tonight, I confess that your hand is powerful. Though your hand is powerful, you allowed it to be pierced for me. Out of love, you laid down your life so that I might live. Thank you for dying for me. Because of your death and resurrection, I can approach your "throne of grace with confidence" tonight (Heb. 4:16).

So, tonight, I call to you whose hand is mighty. I ask you to uphold me by your powerful hand. Guide me through valleys of life with your hand. Provide for me and my family "according to the riches of [your] glory" (Phil. 4:19). Vanquish the enemy as he tries to attack me and those I love. Protect my church by your mighty hand. Accomplish miracles among your people with your powerful hand. By your hand, preserve the unity of fellowship in my church. Support the ministers of my church by your powerful hand. Establish the work of my hands as I serve you (Ps. 90:17). Tear down obstacles that keep me from accomplishing your will. By your hand, embolden missionaries as they advance the gospel around the world. I thank you for the day when you will extend your mighty hand to "wipe away every tear" from my eyes (Rev. 7:17). Tonight, I rest, Lord, underneath your powerful, almighty hand.

Day 40 — Morning

And I Will Praise

*I long for your salvation, Oh Lord,
and I meditate on your law.*
*May my soul live and I will praise you,
and may your judgments help me.*
—Psalm 119:174–175

Meditation is not the carefree mental exercise of those who don't have a concern in the world. It is not simply the antidote for stress on days when you need to relax. Instead, it is the practice of those who wait desperately for the Lord to answer prayer. It is peace for those who endure satanic assaults. It is the lifeline of those who want to remain faithful to Christ in the midst of harrowing circumstances. It is spiritual aid for believers who have determined that they will remain faithful "even to the point of death" (Rev. 2:10). It is the practice of those who understand how capable they are of falling into temptation. It is the joy of those who erupt in the loudest praise. It is the wartime strategy of soldiers who have decided to stand firm against the "powers of this dark world and against the spiritual forces of evil in the heavenly realms" (Eph. 6:12). Meditating on God's Word is powerful and life-changing.

For forty days you have fixed your hearts and minds on Scripture. You have studied and meditated on God's Word. Every morning and every night, you have drawn near to Christ by feasting on the divine banquet of Scripture. For forty days you have worshipped, prayed, and confessed sin. Let me ask you a simple question: What has God done in your life during this time? How has the Lord blessed you? I feel confident that the Lord has ministered to you in powerful ways. I know that the Lord has taught you, encouraged you, comforted you, strengthened you, and helped you in countless ways. God's Word never returns void, but always accomplishes the purpose for which it was sent (Isa. 55:11).

What if you could experience the intimacy you've had with Jesus over the last forty days for the rest of your life? How might God bless you if you continued to spend time with the Lord every morning and every night? How might this regular time in God's Word positively impact your relationships, your family, and your future? Maybe God will use you in mighty ways to bless your brothers and sisters in Christ. Or perhaps the Lord will call you to do incredible things that you never dreamt possible. Maybe God will use you in powerful ways to advance the gospel around the world. But you will never know what you missed out on if you stop meditating on God's Word.

Decide right here and now that you will seek Christ relentlessly through His Word. Not out of obligation but out of love for the Lord, plant your life in the Scripture. Choose to be among the small minority of those who experience the blessed life, the very concept that the psalmist began with (Ps. 119:1–2). You cannot stand to miss out on the blessings of seeking Christ relentlessly in His Word!

Lost Sheep

*I have strayed as a lost sheep; seek your servant
because I have not forgotten your commandments.*
—Psalm 119:176

Lord, you are my shepherd. You make me lie down in green
pastures, you lead me beside quiet waters, you restore my soul, and
you guide me in paths of righteousness. You comfort me with your rod
and staff (Ps. 23:1–4). You are the Good Shepherd who laid down your
life for me (John 10:11). Yet despite your goodness to me, I confess the
ways in which I have strayed from you.

I confess that I have doubted the goodness of your faithful
guidance. When my journey feels long, I find myself wondering
whether or not you are still leading me. And when I arrive to the
pastures where you bring me, I grow weary of your provision. In
my ingratitude, I become easily distracted and long for pastures that
you have not led me to. I also confess that I sometimes doubt your
powerful rod and staff. I get scared when I see all of the things that
could devour me in the world. I also confess that I get frustrated with
some of the other sheep in my flock. I know that you love them and
died for them as well, but I find it so difficult to extend grace to them.
So I wander from the sweetness of your voice and experience all of
the pain and hurt that you tried so hard to protect me from. But,
thankfully, you do not treat me as my sins deserve.

No matter how far I stray from your voice, you always seek after me. Thank you for leaving the "ninety-nine" to rescue me from my folly (Luke 15:4– 6). Come after me in love when I become prideful and selfish. Seek me when I wander towards bitterness and anger. Find me when I am lost in fear and doubt. Come after me when I'm seeking the wrong company. And when you call after me, I will hear your voice and follow my Shepherd. Your sheep always hear your voice (John 10:16). Thank you for being my Shepherd. Thank you for letting me be one of your sheep. Help me to relentlessly follow you through your Word.

Next Steps to a Relentless Life

1. Don't Stop. Over the last forty days, you have grown accustomed to starting and ending every day with the Lord. Each morning you read and meditated on God's Word. Every night you prayed God's Word back to Him. If you relax these habits, even for a day, you risk losing something very precious that you worked hard to establish. Don't stop. A relentless life never stops seeking, praying, and studying God's Word. Set your alarm so that you will wake up in plenty of time to spend time in God's Word in the morning. In the evening, turn off the television, shut down your tablet, put your phone down, and close out the day by praying God's Word back to Him. This book is not simply about a forty-day experience, it's about achieving a relentless life!

2. Stay in Community. You will never be able to pursue Christ relentlessly on your own. If you have committed to a small group over the course of your study of Psalm 119, stay in it. If you have joined a church as a result of this study, faithfully attend. However well-intentioned and disciplined you are, your commitment will eventually fade without the support and encouragement of a Christian community. You need the accountability that only your brothers and sisters in Christ can provide. It is great that we live in a day and age where you can podcast or watch videos of your favorite preachers, but do not think for a moment that this replaces your need to spend time with fellow brothers and sisters in Christ. But even if you could manage your Christian life on your own (which you cannot), your brothers and sisters in Christ need you. Will you be there when

they face disappointment and tragedy? Will they have you to call on when they are going through a difficult time in their marriage? Your life in Christ is not just about you and Jesus. Stay in community.

3. **Teach Others.** You have an obligation to share what you have learned in this study with those who could benefit. Would you consider going through this study with a younger believer in Christ? Do you have a friend, neighbor, or coworker who needs to read this book? Maybe God will lead you to start a small group in your home. Aside from the Christian responsibility, there is something wonderful about passing along what you have learned. You will solidify what you have learned if you take the next step of teaching another person. Teaching others forces you to live what you know and continue to grow in your understanding of Scripture. Those who have no interest in helping others can grow stagnant in their relationship with the Lord. Ask God to show you whom He wants you to teach.

4. **Serve.** There is something about serving that keeps you desperately seeking the Lord. Pouring your life into others makes you hungry for more of God's Word. Over and over this study reminded you that being a member of the body of Christ is about serving your brothers and sisters in Christ. No matter how well they may seem on Sunday morning, all of them have pain and hurt in their lives. While you cannot solve their problems, you can serve them in the midst of their storm. How can you use your spiritual gifts to bless your brothers and sisters in Christ (Rom. 12:6–8)? Pray and ask God how He wants you to serve in your local church.

5. **Witness.** If your fervent study of the Scripture did not produce a desire to share your faith with others, there is a problem. The goal of studying God's Word is never to simply fill your mind with knowledge. God wants you to love Him with all of your heart and your neighbor as yourself. Whom in your life do you need to tell about Jesus Christ? Have you shared your testimony lately? Have you invited your neighbors to church? Are you praying regularly for people to come to Christ? A relentless pursuit of Christ should always translate into witnessing relentlessly to those who do not know the Lord. Does your church have an evangelistic team? If they do, maybe you ought to join them. If they do not, maybe the Lord will lead you to start one. Pray regularly for the Lord to give you an opportunity to share the reason for the hope you have (1 Pet. 3:15).

6. Confess Sin. Regular and intentional confession of sin is a lost discipline in much of the evangelical world. Studying God's Word will continually drive us to confess the ways in which we have failed to live a life that honors the Lord. God is waiting for His children to stop rationalizing their sins and start confessing them. When we confess our sins, God is "faithful and just to forgive us of all unrighteousness" (1 John 1:9). Lead your family, your Bible study, and your church in confession. Confess your sins to each other (James 5:16) and experience the joy of walking in close fellowship with Jesus.

7. Worship. Over the last forty days, you have sunken deep into the heart of a Father whose love for you is beyond comprehension. You have basked in His power and His mercy. You have dwelled on His matchless grace. Over and over you have considered His love displayed on the cross. You have meditated on the power of the resurrection. You have remembered His precious promises to guide, comfort, protect, and care for you. You have contemplated the joy He can give you in sorrow as well as the hope of heaven. Allow all of these glorious realities to drive you to worship Him relentlessly. "Shout for joy … burst into jubilant song with music" (Ps. 98:4). "Give thanks to the LORD, for he is good. His love endures forever" (Ps. 136:1). "Worship the LORD in the splendor of his holiness" (Ps. 96:9). A relentless pursuit of Christ will always result in relentless worship!

"Amen! Praise and glory and wisdom and thanks and honor and power
and strength be to our God for ever and ever. Amen!"
—Revelation 7:12

Memorizing Psalm 119

The fact that the structure of Psalm 119 commends memorization speaks volumes about the worth of God's Word. Imagine the absurdity of memorizing 176 lines of your daily newspaper, favorite blog, or instructional manual at work. Certainly nothing man conjures on his own is worthy of this much attention. But as this Psalm teaches, we are blessed as we immerse ourselves in God's Word and live according to it. I have personally experienced the blessings of memorizing Psalm 119. Few things have wrought more spiritual fruit in my life. No matter where I am throughout the day, I can meditate on God's Word. Whether I'm lying in bed trying to go to sleep or driving down the road, I can spend time in the Bible. And no matter how many times I recite the verses of Psalm 119, God always wants to teach me something new. For those of you who are interested in tackling this challenge, I want to share with you a few things that I learned in the process.

1. Take your Time. It seems like I am always pressed for time. So my general approach for many things in life is "the faster the better." However, committing Psalm 119 to memory is more about spending time in the Psalm than it is about being able to parrot the words back in perfect order. So no matter how long it takes you to memorize the Psalm, you will have succeeded in saturating your mind in Scripture. Now you may be a memory savant with the unusual ability to memorize enormous amounts of information in a short period of time, but most likely it is going to be very hard for you, like it was for me. Commit yourself to memorizing one verse at a time. Don't

try to cram the verses into your head; you will only become frustrated. There are no shortcuts to memorizing 176 verses. If you hurry unnecessarily and cheat the process, you will quickly forget the verses. Plus, you may get terribly confused, given the interchangeable usage of eight very similar words. The length and complexity of Psalm 119 requires that you take your time. Try to master each octet before moving on to the next.

2. **Always Have a Bible with You.** Take a Bible with you wherever you go so that you can work on your memorization no matter where you are. It is very challenging to rehearse the verses when you don't have a way to check yourself for accuracy. If you are not consistently checking yourself for accuracy, you may be committing the wrong words to memory. It can take a while to unlearn the wrong wording and relearn the correct wording of the verses. With that in mind, always use the same translation. Memorizing Psalm 119 is difficult enough without the added challenge of being confused by the various ways in which translations render the Hebrew. A great alternative to bringing your whole Bible with you is creating verse cards that can be packed neatly into your pocket. Verse cards work great for drilling your memory work, but it may be difficult for you to keep track of 176 separate pieces of paper. You can also use your smart phone or tablet if you find it more convenient.

3. **Review Aloud.** If you don't use it, you will lose it. Along with the task of memorizing comes the equally important task of reviewing what you have committed to memory. You will need to spend equal time on both tasks. Try reading the verses aloud that you have memorized every day. If you do this consistently, the verses will slowly become a part of you. When you are close to mastering the verses, try covering them up and reciting them from memory while you look only at the verse numbers. This will help you solidify the connection between the verses and the verse numbers, and it only takes a few minutes. One of the greatest benefits to saying the verses aloud is that it helps the muscles in and around your mouth develop muscle memory. Have you ever seen a pianist rapidly play from one end of the keyboard to the other? Such a feat is possible not because they are thinking about each note before they play it, but because they have trained their fingers to remember the sequence. Over time, executing the sequence of notes becomes as natural as breathing. So it is with verbalizing Scripture. You can literally teach your lips, mouth, and tongue to remember what it feels like to say the verses of Psalm 119. Without having to think about each verse, you can get to the point where muscle memory takes over.

4. **Review Silently.** I also recommend rehearsing the verses silently in your mind. Early on in the process, it may help you to visualize each verse as you recite it internally. After a while, however, you will find yourself rehearsing the verses at a rate faster than you can speak. If I know the stanza really well, it only takes me about twelve seconds to mentally review it. This technique works great when you don't have light to read or when you have to be quiet, like at night. I have fallen asleep countless times rehearsing the words of Psalm 119 in my head. What a great way to live the words of verse 55, "I remember in the night your name, Oh Lord, and I will keep your law."

5. **Review on Paper.** You may find it helpful to write the verses from memory in your journal. Writing the verses has the benefit of forcing you to slow down and think about the things you are memorizing. As you meticulously write down the verses you are working on, God will likely open your mind to understand them on a deeper level, a process that will fuel your prayers and worship for the day. If you don't like writing, try typing. Typing is still slower than speaking, and it gives you the opportunity to reinforce your memory in a tangible way.

6. **Master the First Verse of Each Octet.** It will be very difficult to memorize 176 verses in sequence without using the structure of the Psalm as a guide. I highly recommend mastering the first verse of each octet so that you will be able to mentally track where you are in Psalm 119 as you recite the verses. When I choose a random verse to recite, I often have to figure out which octet it belongs to before I can say the verse. Without these "verse hangers" it is really tough to memorize the verses. Ultimately, the goal is to develop such a close relationship with each individual verse that you don't need to locate it within an octet in order to recite it, but this level of mastery takes time.

7. **Give Equal Attention to the Second Half of the Psalm.** In my quest to memorize Psalm 119, I found that the first half of the Psalm was much easier for me than the second half. Since verse 1 is the logical starting place, I spent much more time reviewing the opening verses than the later ones. I would recommend that you force yourself to rehearse the second half of the Psalm every bit as much as the first half. You might even practice reciting *Tav* to *Alef* in descending order.

8. Recite Portions of the Psalm Publicly. Having the opportunity to recite some of the verses publically gives you the added motivation to work hard in your memorization. As long as we are doing it for the right reason, it can inspire your brothers and sisters in Christ to commit God's Word to memory. The verses that I have prepared for public recitation are burned into my mind. I simply do not know the rest of Psalm 119 as well as those verses. Ask your Sunday school teacher or small group leader to give you an opportunity to recite a couple of stanzas from memory. Or maybe your pastor can include the Scripture recitation in one of your upcoming worship services.

9. Identify and Drill the Difficult Verses. The biggest challenge in Psalm 119 is to remember the nuances of verses that are very similar to each other. It becomes difficult to remember which verse says, "give me life according to your word" (v. 107) and which one says, "give me life according to your law" (v. 50). Then there are some verses which, for whatever reason, just will not stick in your head. These challenges can be overcome through hard work. But truth be told, I still get tripped up with certain verses. Identify the difficult verses and spend much more time drilling them.

10. Play Number Games. I like to play number games with Psalm 119. Here is an example: Pick a random number, recite the verse; then add twenty and recite the verse. Next, take away three, then recite the verse; then add fifty and recite the verse: I think you get the picture. Here's something else you can try. Start with verse 2 and recite the second verse of each octet all the way through the Psalm. In other words, add eight to every verse you recite. Repeat this process, but start with verse 3, then 4, all the way to verse 8. You can also ask somebody in your family to randomly call out verses for you to recite. This will force you to keep refining the memory work you have already done. This process will also identify passages within the Psalm that you do not know very well.

Translation of Psalm 119

א

1. Blessed are those whose ways are blameless,
    who walk according to the law of the Lord.
2. Blessed are those who keep his testimonies,
    with all of their heart they seek him.
3. They also do no wrong; they walk in his ways.
4. You have commanded your precepts
    to be kept exceedingly.
5. Oh that my ways may be established
    to keep your statutes.
6. Then I would not be ashamed
    when I consider all of your commandments.
7. I will praise you with an upright heart
    as I learn your righteous judgments.
8. I will keep your statutes;
    do not totally forsake me.

ב

9. How can a young man keep his way pure?
    By keeping it according to your word.
10. With all of my heart I have sought you;
    do not let me stray from your commandments.

11. I have laid up your word in my heart so that I will not sin against you.
12. Blessed are you, Oh Lord, teach me your statutes.
13. With my lips I recount all of the judgments of your mouth.
14. I rejoice in the way of your testimonies as much as in all of the riches.
15. I will meditate on your precepts and I will consider your ways.
16. I delight in your statutes; I will not forget your word.

ג

17. Deal kindly with your servant
    and I will live and I will keep your word.
18. Open my eyes that I may see the wonders of your law.
19. I am a stranger on earth;
    do not hide your commandments from me.
20. My soul wastes with longing
    for your judgments at all times.
21. You rebuke the arrogant who are cursed,
    who stray from your commandments.
22. Remove from me shame and contempt,
    for I have kept your testimonies.
23. Even though rulers sit and speak against me,
    your servant will meditate on your statutes.
24. Your testimonies are my delight,
    my counselors.

ד

25. My soul clings to the dust;
    give me life according to your word.
26. I have recounted my ways
    and you answered me;
    teach me your statutes.
27. Make me understand the way of your precepts
    and I will meditate on all of your wonders.
28. My soul weeps from sorrow;
    strengthen me according to your word.
29. Put away from me the way of deception;
    give me life according to your law.
30. I have chosen the way of faithfulness;
    I have set your judgments before me.
31. I cling to your testimonies, Oh Lord,
    do not let me be put to shame.

32.   I run in the path of your commandments,
      for you have broadened my heart.

ה

33.   Teach me, Oh Lord, the way of your statutes
      and I will keep them to the end.
34.   Give me understanding and I will keep your law
      and obey it with all of my heart.
35.   Lead me in the path of your commandments,
      for in them I delight.
36.   Incline my heart to your testimonies and not to selfish gain.
37.   Turn my eyes from seeing worthless things
      and give me life in your ways.
38.   Establish your word to your servant that you may be feared.
39.   Take away my disgrace which I dread, for your judgments are good.
40.   See how I long for your precepts; in your righteousness, give me life.

ו

41.   May your steadfast love come to me, Oh Lord,
      your salvation according to your word.
42.   Then I will give an answer to the one who taunts me,
      for I trust in your word.
43.   Do not snatch the word of truth utterly from my mouth,
      for I have put my hope in your judgments.
44.   I will keep your law continually,
      forever and ever.
45.   I will walk about in a broad place,
      for I have sought your precepts.
46.   I will speak of your testimonies
      before kings and not be ashamed.
47.   I delight in your commandments
      because I love them.
48.   I lift up my hands unto your commandments
      which I love and I meditate on your statutes.

ז

49.   Remember the word to your servant,
      for I have put my hope in it.
50.   This is my comfort in my affliction,
      that your word gives me life.

51. The arrogant mock me exceedingly,
    but I have not turned from your law.
52. I remember your judgments from of old, Oh Lord,
    and I am comforted by them.
53. Rage seizes me because of the wicked
    who have forsaken your law.
54. Your statutes have been my song
    in the house of my journey.
55. I remember in the night your name,
    Oh Lord, and I will keep your law.
56. This is my practice; I keep your precepts.

ח

57. The Lord is my portion;
    I have promised to keep your word.
58. I have sought your face with my whole heart;
    give me life according to your word.
59. I have considered my ways
    and I have turned my feet unto your testimonies.
60. I will hasten and not delay to keep your commandments.
61. The cords of the wicked have bound me;
    I have not forgotten your law.
62. In the middle of the night,
    I rise to thank you for your righteous judgments.
63. I am a companion to all who fear you,
    to those who keep your precepts.
64. Your steadfast love fills the earth;
    teach me your statutes.

ט

65. You have done good with your servant,
    according to your word, Oh Lord.
66. Teach me knowledge and good judgment,
    for I believe in your commandments.
67. Before I was afflicted I strayed, but now I keep your word.
68. You are good and do good; teach me your statutes.
69. The arrogant have forged lies against me,
    but I will keep your precepts with all of my heart.
70. Their heart is unfeeling as fat, but I delight in your law.
71. It was good for me that I was afflicted
    so that I might learn your statutes.

72.   The law from your mouth is better to me
than thousands of pieces of gold and silver.

י

73.   Your hands made me and formed me;
give me understanding
and I will learn your commandments.
74.   May those who fear you, see me and rejoice
because I have put my hope in your word.
75.   I know, Oh Lord, that your judgments are righteous,
and in faithfulness you have afflicted me.
76.   May your steadfast love comfort me,
according to your word to your servant.
77.   May your compassion come to me and I will live,
for your law is my delight.
78.   May the arrogant be ashamed for they have wronged me falsely;
I will meditate on your precepts.
79.   May those who fear you turn to me,
those who know your testimonies.
80.   May my heart be blameless in your statutes
so that I will not be ashamed.

כ

81.   My soul languishes for your salvation;
I hope in your word.
82.   My eyes fail for your words,
saying, "when will you comfort me?"
83.   For I have been like a wineskin in the smoke;
I have not forgotten your statutes.
84.   How long are the days of your servant?
When will you execute judgment on those who persecute me?
85.   The arrogant dig pits for me, which are not in keeping with your law.
86.   All of your commandments are faithful;
they persecute me falsely—help me.
87.   They almost destroyed me on the earth,
but I have not forsaken your precepts.
88.   According to your steadfast love,
give me life and I will keep the testimonies of your mouth.

ל

89. Forever, Oh Lord, your word is stationed in the heavens.
90. Your faithfulness continues from generation to generation;
   you established the earth and it stands firm.
91. Your judgments stand today,
   for all of them are your servants.
92. If your law had not been my delight,
   then I would have perished in my affliction.
93. Forever, I will not forget your precepts,
   for by them you have given me life.
94. I am yours; save me,
   for I have sought your precepts.
95. The wicked wait to destroy me;
   I will consider your testimonies.
96. To all perfection I have seen an end,
   but your commandments are exceedingly broad.

מ

97. Oh how I love your law;
   I meditate on it all of the day.
98. Your commandments make me wiser than my enemies,
   for they are forever with me.
99. I have more insight than all my teachers,
   for I meditate on your statutes.
100. I have more understanding than the elders,
   because I have kept your precepts.
101. I have withheld my feet from every evil path
   so that I might keep your word.
102. I have not turned away from your judgments,
   for you have taught me.
103. How sweet are your words to my taste,
   more than honey to my mouth.
104. I get understanding from your precepts;
   therefore, I hate every false path.

נ

105. Your word is a lamp to my feet
   and a light for my path.
106. I have taken an oath and confirmed it,
   to keep your righteous judgments.

107. I am exceedingly afflicted, Oh Lord,
     give me life according to your word.
108. Accept, Oh Lord, the willing offering of my mouth
     and teach me your judgments.
109. My life is in my hands continually,
     but I have not forgotten your law.
110. The wicked have set a snare for me,
     but I do not stray from your precepts.
111. I have inherited your testimonies forever,
     for they are the joy of my heart.
112. I have inclined my heart to do your statutes,
     forever to the end.

ס

113. I hate those who are double-minded,
     but I love your law.
114. You are my hiding place and my shield;
     I put my hope in your word.
115. Go away from me evildoers,
     that I may keep the commandments of my God.
116. Sustain me according to your word and I will live;
     do not let me be ashamed from my hope.
117. Uphold me and I will be delivered;
     I will look on your statutes continually.
118. You reject all who stray from your statutes,
     for their deceitfulness is deception.
119. You discard all of the wicked of the earth like dross;
     therefore, I love your testimonies.
120. My flesh trembles from fear of you
     and I fear your judgments.

ע

121. I have done justice and righteousness;
     do not leave me to my oppressors.
122. Ensure good for your servant;
     do not let the arrogant oppress me.
123. My eyes fail for your salvation
     and for your righteous word.
124. Deal with your servant according to your steadfast love
     and teach me your statutes.

125. I am your servant; give me understanding
that I might know your testimonies.
126. It is time for you to act, Oh Lord,
they have broken your law.
127. Therefore, I love your commandments more than gold,
more than fine gold.
128. Therefore, all of your precepts are upright;
I hate every false path.

פ

129. Your testimonies are wonderful;
therefore, my soul keeps them.
130. The unfolding of your word gives light,
giving understanding to the simple.
131. I open wide my mouth and pant,
for I long for your commandments.
132. Turn to me and be gracious,
as is fitting for those who love your name.
133. Establish my footsteps in your word,
and do not let any iniquity rule over me.
134. Redeem me from the oppression of men
that I may keep your precepts.
135. Cause your face to shine on your servant
and teach me your statutes.
136. Streams of tears pour from my eyes
because they have not kept your law.

ע

137. You are righteous, Oh Lord,
and your judgments are upright.
138. You have commanded your testimonies in righteousness
and in exceeding faithfulness.
139. My zeal consumes me,
for my enemies have forgotten your words.
140. Your word has been tested exceedingly and your servant loves it.
141. I am small and despised;
I have not forgotten your precepts.
142. Your righteousness is an eternal righteousness
and your law is true.

143. Distress and anguish have found me;
     your commandments are my delight.
144. Your testimonies are righteous for eternity;
     give me understanding that I may live.

ק

145. I call with all of my heart: answer me,
     Oh Lord, and I will keep your statutes.
146. I call out to you, save me
     and I will keep your testimonies.
147. I rise early in the morning and I cry for help;
     I have put my hope in your word.
148. My eyes anticipate the night watches,
     to meditate on your word.
149. Hear my voice according to your steadfast love,
     Oh Lord, give me life according to your judgments.
150. Those who pursue evil draw near;
     they are far from your law.
151. You are near, Oh Lord,
     and all of our commandments are true.
152. Long ago I have known from your testimonies
     that you established them for eternity.

ר

153. Look upon my affliction and deliver me,
     for I have not forgotten your law.
154. Plead my cause and redeem me;
     give me life according to your word.
155. Salvation is far from the wicked,
     for they do not seek your statutes.
156. Your compassions are many, Oh Lord,
     give me life according to your judgments.
157. My persecutors and my distress are many;
     I have not turned from your testimonies.
158. I look on the faithless and I loathe them
     because they do not keep your word.
159. See that I love your precepts, Oh Lord,
     give me life according to your steadfast love.
160. All of your words are true
     and all of your righteous judgments are eternal.

שׁ

161. Rulers persecute me without cause,
     but my heart trembles at your word.
162. I rejoice over your words as one who finds great riches.
163. I hate and abhor deception but I love your law.
164. Seven times in the day I praise you
     for your righteous judgments.
165. Great peace have those who love your law
     and nothing makes them stumble.
166. I wait for your salvation, Oh Lord,
     and I do your commandments.
167. My soul keeps your testimonies
     and I love them exceedingly.
168. I keep your precepts and your testimonies,
     for all of my ways are before you.

ת

169. May my cry reach you, Oh Lord,
     give me understanding according to your word.
170. May my supplication come before you;
     deliver me according to your word.
171. My lips will pour out praise,
     for you have taught me your statutes.
172. My tongue will sing of your word,
     for all of your commandments are righteous.
173. May your hand help me,
     for I have chosen your precepts.
174. I long for your salvation, Oh Lord,
     and I meditate on your law.
175. May my soul live and I will praise you,
     and may your judgments help me.
176. I have strayed as a lost sheep; seek your servant
     because I have not forgotten your commandments.

Notes

1. Kevin J. Moore, "The Meaning of the Hebrew Word (תּוֹרָה) in the Book of Psalms" (PhD diss., Southwestern Baptist Theological Seminary, 2012), 241–44.
2. All of the verses from Psalm 119 represent the author's translation. Other biblical material derives from the New International Version, NIV.
3. The translation makes every attempt to render the Hebrew into contemporary English in a manner that is consistent and faithful to the intent of the Hebrew. In some cases this forces the translation to divert from translating in a word-for-word manner and may necessitate adding words not in the original Hebrew. In general, however, the translation preserves the terse nature of the Hebrew verse. In other cases, the translation will break English norms in order to accommodate some critical aspect of the Hebrew. In certain contexts, the translation will reflect a more awkward rendering of the Hebrew in order to convey meaning that could be otherwise lost in translation. The following eight Hebrew words appear next to their translation: (תּוֹרָה) "law"; (עֵדוּת) "testimonies"; (פִּקּוּדִים) "precepts"; (חֹק) "statute"; (מִצְוֹת) "commandment"; (מִשְׁפָּטִים) "judgment"; (אִמְרָה) "word"; (דָּבָר) "word." Though the Hebrew intends eight different words to signify *Torah*, only seven will be used. This is caused by the challenge of finding two English words to convey accurately (אִמְרָה) and (דָּבָר). Some effort was made to preserve the word order of the Hebrew in cases where there seemed to be an emphasis made by the psalmist. This will not be true in every case, since there is also significant concern for the clarity of the English.